Lee Stoneh...
from dad - Dec. 1953

3⁷⁰

Here's a How-de-do

✳·✳·✳✳✳✳✳✳✳✳✳✳✳✳✳✳✳✳✳✳✳✳✳✳✳

Here's a How-de-do

MY LIFE IN
GILBERT & SULLIVAN

By

Martyn Green

W·W·NORTON *&* COMPANY · INC · *New York*

✻✽✻✽✻✽✻✽✻✽✻✽✻✽✻✽✻✽✻✽

Contents

5

✳✳✳✳✳✳✳✳✳✳✳✳✳✳✳✳✳✳✳✳✳✳

Illustrations

7

8 · Here's a How-de-do

Here's a How-de-do

Prologue

When the Savoy Theatre closed its doors after the last per-
formance of the D'Oyly Carte Opera Company's Festival of
Britain season, twenty-seven of the performers left the company, among them Ella Halman, Margaret Mitchell, Richard
Watson, and myself.

Since our decision to leave was made known we have all
been asked over and over again: "What's the matter? Why
are you leaving?"

Those are questions that may never be answered, because
anything I might say would be either disbelieved, discounte-
nanced, or treated as a joke, and I am certain that Ella Halman
saw nothing funny in it at all. All I can say is that we did not
take the step lightly, nor did we take it alone.

As I reread what I have written, I find that a degree of Gil-
bertian bitterness has crept in here and there. This, I suppose,
is only proper, for I have spent thirty years speaking and singing Gilbert's lines, and that Gilbert was at times bitter (and at
nearly all times embittered) there can be no possible doubt, no
possible, probable shadow of doubt, no possible doubt whatever.

Yet I hope the book maintains more of a spirit of lightness
and laughter in keeping with the predominant spirit of both

Gilbert and Sullivan. And indeed this also is only proper, for it has been the predominant spirit of my life, and I trust it will continue to be.

✳✳✳✳✳✳✳✳✳✳✳✳✳✳✳✳✳✳✳✳✳✳✳

ONE

To Begin With

To begin with—I was born. And when you come to think of it, it is as good a way of beginning life as any other. It was on April 22, 1899, that I entered this world as the third child and second son of what was eventually to become a family of four, namely a boy, a girl, myself, and another girl.

William Green, my father, was a singer, a tenor, and I was given my first name William after him. My elder sister was named Patti, after the singer, Madame Adelina Patti. Among the five people after whom my younger sister was named were two famous prima donnas of that time, Madame Albani and Madame Ella Russell, both of whom acted as godmothers.

It was through one of these godmothers, Ella Russell, that I made my first public appearance. Madame Russell was staying in Blackpool, where for many years our family made its head-quarters in summer, and we were visiting her at her hotel. What the occasion was, and how it all came about, I don't now recall, but I do remember myself on the platform of the hotel ballroom before a large gathering, singing my favorite song, "Yes, let me like a soldier fall!" It was probably my favorite song because I had heard my father sing it, and I sang it on every possible occasion; indeed, I was known to make or force the opportunity if I could not see one looming up. Perhaps that is what occurred on this occasion. I'm still very fond of the song, though I have not sung it—except in my bath—for close on forty years.

Over my school days I prefer to draw a veil. The only incident of note is that I once obtained third place in my form. Having done that, I sat back on my laurels and the following week resumed my usual place, which at least had the advantage that I could not go any lower. Having, however, in spite of my scholastic deficiencies, a pleasant soprano voice, I found myself selected for the school choir; it was at this point that I began to realize why I had been permitted to indulge my liking for "Yes, let me like a soldier fall!" Later I graduated from the choir to the special choir, a small but select number of boys possessed of voices above the average—about a dozen all told. This special choir was one of the principal attractions at the annual Speech Day and other functions of a similar nature, at which I appeared with them on several occasions during my stay at the school.

My school days were not destined to be many. In 1912 the death of my elder brother was followed by the long and serious illness of my mother. My father, what with the shock of Alex's death and the worry over Mother's illness, seemed to lose all heart and confidence in himself. Contract after contract was cancelled because of illness brought on by worry; then investments began to go wrong, and our financial position became worse and worse. By the spring of 1913 it was becoming essential that I begin to think of earning, if not a living, at least something that would help to relieve the burden; so I was sent to an uncle in Bolton, who had undertaken to find me a job, which he did—as office boy to a friend of his, an auctioneer and valuer in Bowkers Row. In this capacity I licked and stuck on stamps, copied letters, "cleaned the windows and swept the floor, and polished up the handle on the big front door."

I had not been there long before I discovered that my boss appeared to do very little in the way of auctioneering and about an equal quantity of valuing. He was, however, frequently to be seen going off with a large suitcase. Since he most inconsiderately kept it locked, I had no opportunity of gratifying my curiosity as to its contents until one day he called me into his private sanctum. On entering, I found him seated at his desk with his precious case open before him. My eyes immediately flew to its interior. It was full of—conjuring tricks!

"What do you think of this?" he asked me, and then, without waiting for a reply, proceeded to show me a trick, a very wonderful trick. Taking a lot of coloured silk handkerchiefs, he put them one by one into a little black bag which he had assured me was empty and which he had even turned inside out to prove it, and then pulled them out again all knotted together. Due amazement was registered by me, but when he put them back again and permitted them to untie themselves within the bag, bringing them out single and unattached, I was dumfounded.

"How do you do it, sir?" I enquired eagerly.

"That's my secret," he said, and then added, "It's a new one I've just got. I wanted to try it out before I put it on at a children's party I'm doing this afternoon."

So that was his murky secret. That was why I was learning so little about auctioneering and valuing. He was a conjurer at children's parties. Never was a boy's curiosity so nearly completely satisfied. I say "nearly" because it never will be satisfied completely. To this day I don't know how that trick was done. I rather hope I never do.

I didn't stay long with him—not more than a few months. Somehow I did not take kindly to his particular form of auctioneering (not that I would have taken kindly to any form of it), and eventually I moved on to the firm of Messrs. J. Pendlebury & Co. in Wigan, one of the largest stores in that town, where I became an articled apprentice to the drapery trade. Someone had persuaded my mother that "business training" would stand me in good stead throughout life, whether I continued in the business or not. Personally I suspect that whoever it was had some sort of interest in the firm, and merely wanted to get an assistant that they need not pay a wage to.

I was still at Pendlebury's when the First World War broke out. From that fatal day in August, 1914, when we, as a country, found ourselves at grips with Germany for the first time, the urge to "do my bit," in spite of my somewhat tender years, daily grew stronger within me. Of course, it could have been that I had contracted "khaki fever"—a peculiar and virulent disease that evidenced itself by way of a sharp pain every time you saw a fellow in uniform, especially if you both happened to be passing the same girl and she looked and smiled at him in preference to you!

Whatever the reason, as soon as the winter sale was over, at the end of January, 1915, I went in to the managing director and told him I intended to join the army. I was promptly told I was not to do anything of the kind. I was "too young"—which was true, but seemed to me to be one more reason for joining up; I was becoming a little fed up with being an apprentice. However, I didn't mention this sentiment, and returned to my department a disappointed but subdued youth.

Towards the end of March, two of the other apprentices, apparently with permission, enlisted, and all my old urge returned with renewed vigour. I became more and more restless and dissatisfied, until on Sunday, April 18, just four days before I turned sixteen, two of my friends and I walked into the local recruiting office, told whacking great lies regarding our respective ages (I put mine down as nineteen and four days), and were duly examined, measured, interrogated, sworn in, and given "the King's shilling." We were also given orders to report to the station on the Tuesday morning at 8:15 A.M., to be taken under the wing of an N.C.O. and escorted to Aldershot. I had enlisted in the Army Service Corps.

Having "taken the shilling," I thought there was nothing much the firm could do about it, and once again bearded the managing director. Once again I was given a most emphatic No. I explained as firmly as I could that I had actually enlisted, had "taken the shilling."

"I don't give a damn if you've taken a dozen shillings," he shouted at me. "You're not going—and those are *my* orders!"

"But," I protested, "we've got orders to proceed to Aldershot by the early morning train tomorrow."

At that he completely blew up, called me "a little whippersnapper," and threw me out of his office with a final snort and a "We'll see about that!"

The following morning, instead of going to the shop I went to the station. Since I was not due at the shop until 8:15 and the train left at 8:30, I hoped my absence would not be noticed at once. Nevertheless I was somewhat nervous until I was actually in the train and on the move, fearing someone might have spotted my absence and come along to the station to prevent my departure. As we were steaming out I stuck my head out of the window and saw the head cashier, an elderly, partially bald, grey-haired, pink-cheeked, muttonchop-whiskered gentleman, running down the platform after the train as if he would pull me out by the scruff of my neck. I grinned cheekily and blew him a soldier's farewell. The last I saw of him he was standing puffing on the platform, shaking an impotent fist at my fast-disappearing figure. And that, thought I, was that!

We reached Aldershot that evening, went through the normal formalities of reception, and were eventually shown to our barracks. The next day was spent in being kitted, inoculated, interrogated, vaccinated, re-interrogated, lectured, and taught how to salute. The evening was our own, and that was spent in scrounging round among all the other recruits in the hope of finding something in the way of boots, tunic, or trousers that would fit, and making a swap.

The next morning we were paraded along with a large number of other recruits, wondering what was in store for us that morning. Visions of dealing with vast quantities of stores and rations and generally providing the whole of the British Expeditionary Force with the means of winning the war flitted through my mind as we awaited instructions. We got them. We were detailed off for various fatigues. I found myself carrying a broom and shovel and accompanying two other fellows and a barrow with instructions to brush and clean the camp streets. At that time the army was not motorized.

After a few weeks I was sent to the north of England, where I formed part of the supply unit to the Northumberland Fusiliers, stationed some eight miles out of Newcastle-on-Tyne. It was while I was stationed there that the blow fell—about the first week in August. I was summoned one day to the O.C.'s tent-cum-office—we were and had been living under canvas for some time. He asked my age, and when I gave it as nineteen and four months, though he didn't actually call me a liar he gave me to understand that he considered it some distance from the truth. Within a week I was bunged off to Derby, where I spent two days before being ignominiously flung out on my ear.

It appeared that the head cashier of Pendlebury's, realizing that there was not much he could do to stop me the morning of my departure, as I was already in a moving train, had gone straight back to the managing director. This gentleman had then gone to the recruiting office and filed an application for my release on the grounds that I was an apprentice to his firm bound by articles of indenture—and furthermore, well below the required age. On looking back, I must admit I cannot think of any sounder reasons.

It also appeared that Pendlebury's idea was that I should return to them and complete the conditions of the indentures. But that I definitely decided against. After some considerable discussion, they eventually agreed to release me from my indentures on payment of eight guineas.

I had not been back in Civvy Street a week before I had been stopped three or four times and presented with a white feather by fanatical women—the sort of women who would have called you unpatriotic if you owned a dachshund or played Mendelssohn or Beethoven. On one occasion an extremely healthy-looking man of no more than thirty-two or -three, seeing my A.S.C. cap badge, which I was wearing in the lapel of my coat, stopped me rudely and suggested that I would do better if I wore it in a khaki cap. Each approach rendered me speechless with rage, but it was no use trying to explain, as the particular type would not believe you—not in those fairly early days of the war. I had tried it once, with the result that in no time I found I was dealing, not with one, but with a whole crowd, who followed me jeering and booing as I moved off down the street.

It began to get under my skin and set me wondering if, and how, I could get back into the army. It would mean a couple of lies, I thought. One, my age, and two, that I had not served in the army before. I would not be able to show my discharge certificate, for though I held documents to prove that I was no longer bound by any indentures, it would give away my age. I'd probably have to give a false name as well, I thought. That rather set me back a bit, as I knew that penalties were pretty heavy for false statements.

Returning home after one particularly enraging encounter with fanatical females, I despondently pulled out my discharge certificate, and began to read it. Up to that moment I had not read it properly. And then I saw my way out. Whoever had made out the certificate had failed to realise that if I was discharged for "not having fulfilled the conditions of an indenture"—which was the reason given—I must be under age. My delight knew no bounds when, on reading it through, I saw that my age had been put down as 19 years, 165 days—the age I had given on attestation plus.

There was no longer any reason for me to tell lies to re-enlist. I could produce my discharge certificate without a qualm, for I was in possession of a document covering my release from those "conditions of an indenture." Without more ado, other than informing my mother of my intention and obtaining the necessary two references, I went to the recruiting office at the town hall and re-enlisted in the University and Public Schools Brigade of the Royal Fusiliers. After four months I could once again hold my head high.

I was posted to the 29th Battalion, the reserve battalion for the 20th and 21st Battalions, which formed part of the U.P.S. Brigade, and were already under orders to proceed overseas. Volunteers were called for to go overseas with the parent battalion, and I was among those who came forward. But just before we were to leave, my age was again called into question and I was given the choice of being relegated to "the drums" or receiving temporary discharge and returning to Civvy Street until such time as I was recalled under the first draft plan, the "Derby Scheme," which was just coming into operation. I chose the "Drums," exchanged my title of private for that of drummer, and my rifle for a bugle and piccolo.

Early in 1917 I was promoted to lance corporal. When I learned of my promotion I was stationed in Edinburgh, and had just finished a twenty-four-hour spell of guard duty as guard bugler. Tired as I was, as it had been a pretty sticky spell of duty, I spent the next two and a half hours in sewing on my stripes and the following two and a half parading around so that everybody could see them; and I was distinctly annoyed that chaps seemed to show more interest in what had happened during my twenty-four hours at the castle than in my newborn authority.

Playing a piccolo and blowing a bugle were not the sum total of my musical activities during those First World War years. I had begun to realise that I was the possessor of a not unpleasant baritone voice, though I do not remember my voice breaking. I began to collect some songs—just the usual type of song or ballad that is so dear to the heart of the young singer, but nevertheless a type of song that can still hold its own amid the sentimental slush of today's popular songs. I became a member of the Battalion Glee Party, and appeared with them at many concerts. Occasionally I was raised to the eminence of a soloist.

Eventually my sojourn in Edinburgh came to an end. April of 1917 saw me on my way to Dover, where I remained for a while as a recruit instructor. From Dover I was sent to Mansfield on attachment to a training reserve battalion, once more as instructor, then back to Dover, where I was sent on a signalling course. And in typical army fashion, when I was halfway through the course I was suddenly recalled, together with some half-dozen of the others, and thirty-six hours later we found ourselves huddled in the hold of a cross-Channel troopship en route for Boulogne and Etaples.

So at last I was overseas. This visit lasted something short of a year and was spent mostly on the Cambrai, La Bassée, and Arras fronts. It ended when I picked up a "blighty one" on the night of June 6, 1918.

We had "been out" for three weeks doing some rather intensive training for a big push—the final push, as it happened—though at the time I couldn't see how we'd ever manage to push anything, however small, for we were sadly under strength—we numbered some 350 to 400 to the battalion, whereas full strength was 1,000.

Nevertheless we set off up the line early in the morning of June 6, to relieve a battalion of the Guards. Some little way behind the front line we were met by our guides, who told us we were going into a really cushy sector. In the six weeks they had been there they had had only one casualty. Jerry was over a thousand yards away and the only thing he ever did was to drop a couple of rounds into the centre of a village in No Man's Land twice a day, morning and night. Well, that night he changed his tactics. Within two minutes of our arriving at support trenches he started to throw everything he had at us. It was far from healthy on top, so we dropped into the trench to continue our progress there. But we had not gone more than two dozen paces when he sent over a salvo of three, and the third one dropped right in the middle of us.

My mind is very hazy as to what happened after that. I seem to remember cursing the man in front of me for falling across my knee and twisting it rather badly, and the man on my left for flinging his arms about and knocking my tin hat off. Then I tried to move and found I couldn't. The thought struck me that I must be partially buried. Then I heard a lot of groans.

About a year later, or so it seemed, when the dust and muck had cleared off a bit, I caught the sound of myself groaning and wondered why the hell I was doing that. Suddenly I realized that I had better do something about the whole business. From what I could see, it looked a pretty sort of shambles and it seemed that a few shovels would be necessary, so I began to extricate myself. I noticed that my left arm wasn't much use, and that my left knee was throbbing where that fool in front had fallen on it. Suddenly I was free, and I rushed round the corner of the trench calling for spades. The sergeant of the platoon that had been following us was in the next fire bay attending to a casualty.

"What do you want—are you hit?" he asked.

"No," I said. "But spades to start digging—"

And with that I promptly fell flat on my face. It turned out that my left arm had been rendered useless by several shell splinters in my shoulder, and my twisted left knee held another fair-sized lump of steel that had bored its way through the joint. Apart from these two wounds there was a further piece in my hand, and several more all down my left side. No, I wasn't hit!

Only one other man of my platoon escaped. We waited in a funk-hole until just before daybreak, but no stretchers could be found. What few we had, had gone up with the rest of the platoon. The other man had received a wound, a bad one, in his left hand, but he could still walk, and after some consultation it was decided that we should make some effort to get back down the line by ourselves. He had two good legs and a good hand and arm, and I had one good leg and one good arm, so we ought to be able to make it between us; and anyway, if we waited any longer our chances of getting back that day would be practically nil. So off we went. How we managed it I don't know, but we actually covered some three miles before reaching the advance dressing station.

From that moment on, my progress to hospital was on the flat of my back. Eventually I reached the casualty clearing station at Frevent, where I soon found myself on the operating table. When I came to, it was to find myself encased in a Thomas splint from thigh to sole of foot, with an extension beyond, my arm in a sling, my body a mass of bandages, my head in a near-by church belfry with all the bells ringing, and my stomach in an uproar. My head and stomach eventually returned to normal, but my leg, arm, and body remained encased in their bandages for many a day to come.

Two days after the operation I was sent to a base general hospital at Rouen, a move involving a sixteen-hour journey in a French hospital train. Without doubt that was the most uncomfortable journey I have ever made. The wearer of a

Thomas splint and extension is, apart from any wounds or injuries, completely and utterly helpless so far as that particular limb is concerned, and the whole contraption has to be anchored, when in transit, to the stretcher to prevent it from sliding off. Whether all French hospital trains were built like this one I do not know. The berths or stretcher racks were built across the train, and the train itself swayed from side to side in a most alarming fashion. As may readily be seen, one's body will respond to the swaying of the train in the normal manner, but unfortunately the stretcher upon which one is lying will not, being well secured to a rigid framework that is part of the already springless chassis of the coach. The resultant discomfort, especially if one portion of one's anatomy is securely lashed to the stretcher, plus the ultimate effect of sixteen hours of it upon the injuries within the splint, may be readily imagined.

But even French hospital train journeys come to an end, and at last I arrived at the general hospital at Rouen, where I remained for some three or four weeks. At the end of that time the Medical Officer asked what I thought of "Blighty." I told him in no uncertain terms, and praise be, he marked my case sheet "Considered fit for evacuation to the U.K."

This involved another train journey of some five or six hours, but I didn't care. I was taken from the hospital at three o'clock the following morning and loaded into a waiting ambulance some hundred yards away. It was drizzling, and I caught one of the severest colds I've ever had. The train, thank God, was English, though I wouldn't have cared if it had been a cattle truck; I was on my way home to Blighty. Being an awkward stretcher case (it took four men to carry me instead of the normal two), I was the last aboard the train.

All the berths were full, and I was just left on the floor. And still I didn't care.

When we arrived at Boulogne, I was again the last to be carried aboard the hospital ship, and again all the stretcher racks were full and all the floor space taken up. There was, however, one empty cot, so they transferred me to that, unlashing my splint from the stretcher and, after they had got me on the cot, relashing it to the foot rail of the cot. This cot was, of course, like all the others, bolted to the deck to prevent any impromptu wanderings in the event of rough weather. On the whole, I found myself pretty comfortable, although a little restless at the long wait before sailing time.

About half an hour before we were due to sail, one of the orderlies rolled up with a singularly uncomfortable-looking cork life jacket.

"Come on, chum," said he, "try and sit up and we'll put this on."

"What is it?" I enquired. "And why do I have to put it on?"

"It's a life jacket," he informed me. "Everybody has to wear 'em at sea. You never know," he added brightly, "we might be torpedoed!"

At this moment the ship's M.O. came up. "What's the trouble?" he enquired.

I indicated the life jacket, my leg lashed to the cot, and the screws securing the cot to the deck.

"If we *are* torpedoed, sir," I asked, "what am I expected to do—keep the bloody ship afloat?"

I did not wear the life jacket that trip.

✳✳✳✳✳✳✳✳✳✳✳✳✳✳✳✳✳✳✳✳✳✳✳

T W O

Miracles Do Happen

November 11, 1918. To those of my generation that is a date to remember, and how very well I remember it! I was in hospital at the time, a military hospital near Liverpool specializing in orthopedic work. After my return to England I had spent some months lying on my back in a hospital at Woking but had eventually been allowed to get up. That was an adventure.

After several months in bed, feeling fit as a fiddle and raring to go, one is apt to forget that one's uninjured muscles have become a little flabby. As for the injured members, they are practically atrophied. The day it was decided that I might get up, and the crutches were brought to my bedside, a buzz of expectation went round the ward. Several of the patients present had been there much longer than I and had seen the procedure before. At the time I thought they were merely being sympathetic. Little did I know that a recognised star turn was about to appear. They knew what was going to happen—and it did.

A pair of crutches, a pair of nurses. My legs were gently swung out of the bed and lowered to the floor. Very carefully

I was lifted to an upright position, taking my weight on my uninjured leg, and there supported by one of the nurses while the other placed the crutches under my arms. By this time every eye in the ward was on me.

"Now," said the nurse who appeared to be the one in control. Control! "Swing forward through the crutches and let your good leg come down here," pointing to a spot a yard or more in front of me. Full of confidence, I swung, but somehow I didn't get through. I remained poised in mid-air, supported in some degree by the crutches, for a fraction of a second and promptly fell straight back onto the bed. The only person who did not seem to think it funny was myself. Shouts of laughter from all over the ward greeted my effort. Even the nurses were laughing.

I wasn't allowed to sit back and be annoyed or commiserate with myself. For the next five minutes I was forced to try the thing over and over again—still without much success. Then I was allowed back to my bed—and never has bed been so welcome. The next day further practise took place until I was eventually able to make my way as far as the bathroom, and even got so far as giving myself a bath. In a very short while I was quite able to go out on my crutches into the streets of the town.

That condition had not been long achieved when I was transferred from Woking to Southport, where very shortly after I arrived I received a visit from my father, who, looking very stern, demanded an explanation as to why I had failed to answer my calling-up papers. They had apparently arrived some two weeks before and both the military and the civil police had been to my home with the object of arresting me for not obeying the summons.

From Southport I was again transferred, this time to the Alderhey Orthopedic Hospital, Liverpool, where I was very quickly told that I would probably never walk again without artificial aid, and a most complicated form of hinged splint was designed and made for me. Personally I didn't think much of it, but orders is orders, and I wore it—but only for as long as it took me to get out of sight of any form of authority, when it promptly came off and went under my mattress. I don't think I took the doctors' verdict very seriously—and in any case, at that time I was far too grateful for having come home alive to take such a verdict any other way than philosophically. Of course, they put me on a course of treatment which included hand massage—by an extremely attractive brunette; I enjoyed that—and electrical massage and radiant heat.

Nine o'clock every morning except Sunday found me lying on the massage plinth undergoing hand treatment, and November 11, 1918, was no exception. As usual I was indulging in badinage with Billy, the masseuse. I never found out her real name.

It was a large ward, the massage ward, accommodating some two dozen hand masseuses, not to mention the electrical plinths and radiant heat baths. Every plinth and bath was occupied, including the full-length radiant heat bath, a contraption that looked something like an oversize baby's wicker cradle, fitted inside with about two dozen or more electric bulbs. Conversation was general and no different from any other morning, when one of those sudden silences descended and through the absolute quiet a nursing sister who had come into the ward could be heard saying, "But it's true—it comes to an end at eleven o'clock today."

"What comes to an end?" shouted one of the patients.

"The WAR!" called out the sister.

No one believed her, and she was told in a variety of ways to try pulling the other leg. But her excitement gradually convinced us all that she must be telling the truth. But we were still a little doubtful and demanded to know how she knew. She explained.

"It came through to the Commandant just before nine o'clock. I was in his office with the matron and heard it. An armistice has been signed and fighting comes to an end at eleven o'clock. I wasn't supposed to tell anyone until eleven, but who could keep news like that a secret!" She stopped a moment and there was dead silence—then she could contain herself no longer. "We've won the war," she shouted—and burst into tears.

Then came pandemonium. For the first time my interest in the brunette who massaged me was non-existent. I seized my crutches, grabbed my cap, nearly fell off the plinth in my hurry to get off—Billy remonstrating with me, trying to hold me back, as I thought, but I would have none of it—and set off towards the door in a series of leaps through my crutches followed by long hops. I reached the door and was just about to go through when I realized why Billy had tried to hold me back. I very slowly returned to the plinth, smiled at her rather sheepishly—and put on my trousers.

Fully clothed at last, I made a more sober and, as far as crutches will allow, dignified exit and went to my own ward. I had an idea! When I got to the ward it seemed that every patient there, except the bed cases and those unable to move about other than in a wheel chair, had the same idea. Every one was "poshing himself up." Within half an hour patients were to be seen streaming out of the hospital gates and making their way to the tram terminus at the end of Alderhey Road.

I think the Liverpool Corporation must have anticipated the exodus, for as one tram drove away another drew in, filled up, and drove off in its wake. But they were all going into Liverpool. At the time, my parents were living in Bolton, some forty-odd miles distant. It was possible to reach Bolton by means of a tram going via St. Helens. Several others, about nine all told, had their homes in a similar direction, and it was our intention to get to these homes of ours by means of the trams. It would take longer than by rail, we knew, but it had this advantage: wounded and hospitalized servicemen were permitted to travel free of charge on many of the tramway routes—and the St. Helens Corporation route was one of them. We trusted that the other routes we would have to take would be as generous.

We got to St. Helens in time to be told that the whole of the tramway system from there on had decided, like ourselves, to call it a holiday—and the last one had just stopped running. Well, that was that. We were stranded in St. Helens. Nine of us, including two minus an arm apiece and four on crutches, one of whom was minus both legs.

A passing Royal Mail van came to our assistance. The driver and a couple of bystanders helped us all to mount to the top of the van. In that way we were carried on for many more miles. I eventually reached Bolton and my home around midnight, finishing the journey in a Foden Steam Waggon. I had to wake my family up, and when my mother saw me she promptly had a dozen fits. She calmed down when I spoke. Heaven knows what she thought she saw; I've never found out, but it must have been something awful. I was black with soot from the smoke of the Steam Waggon.

I remained at home—absent without leave, of course—for

the next seven days. On my return to the hospital I was promptly called on the carpet. One would have imagined by the way the commandant ticked me off that I was the only man in the whole of the army to have taken seven days' leave. But I was eventually let go with a warning not to do it again. "You can't slaughter the whole company."

When next I made my way to the massage ward I learned that the patient who had been undergoing radiant heat treatment in the full-length bath had been completely forgotten. Under the influence of the heat generated by the dozen or so electric bulbs, he had fallen asleep and had heard nothing of the announcement. Twelve hours later, seeing a rather strong light burning in the ward when it should have been in complete darkness, a passing night nurse went in to investigate the cause and found the patient sleeping, perhaps rather more heavily than a baby, and in a bath of perspiration, but otherwise none the worse.

I eventually managed to wangle myself a job in the whirlpool baths male massage section. All I had to do in this job was to check in the patients as they reported for treatment, to see that no one missed any, a job that started at 10 A.M. and was over by noon. The rest of the day was my own (I took my own treatment from 8 to 8:45 A.M., and had a very attractive masseuse to give me the same, to boot). By virtue of my job I was permitted to wear khaki, instead of the rather unbecoming hospital blue, and was given a permanent pass up to midnight instead of the usual 7 P.M.—a pass of which I took full advantage.

I was finally discharged from the hospital the following January, given seven days' hospital leave, my crutches, a rail-

way pass to my home, and a further one to enable me to proceed to Hounslow "for final disposition."

The Southern Maid, a George Edwardes (Daly's Theatre
Company) show was playing in Manchester at the time, with
José Collins as Teresa. Robert Evett, the managing director
of the George Edwardes Company, was a very good friend of
my father's, and I had known him since early childhood. At
one time he had been principal tenor in several of the Gilbert
and Sullivan revivals in the early part of the century. He did,
in fact, once bring Gilbert to our house in London. I cannot
claim to remember the occasion, or my sitting on his knee. But
if I did, and I have no reason to doubt the word of my inform-
ant, then I obviously cannot have found Gilbert quite the
ogre he is often made out to be. But then I only met him that
once—so far as I know.

I had for some time shown signs of having a voice and had
also for some time been making up my mind that I would like
to go on the stage. To this end I persuaded my father to take
me over to Manchester and use his influence to get me into one
of Evett's companies. Evett, unfortunately, was not there, and
to make it worse, was not expected to be there until after my
leave had expired. There was only one thing to do—make an
appointment with him as early as possible after he arrived back,
and then wire for an extension of leave. The earliest the appointment could be made was for five days after my seven
days expired, so I wired for seven days' extension. It was refused. That left me with two alternatives: either to let the
appointment go and report to Hounslow on time, and lose
the chance of a job on my return to Civvy Street; or take the
seven days, get the job—I never for one moment doubted I

would—and chance whether I would be out of prison in time to take it up. I chose the latter course.

Dead on time, I kept the appointment. Evett was very glad to see both my father and me, but a queer look came into his eye when he heard what it was all about.

"How do you expect to go on the stage on crutches?" he asked me. "You have to be able to walk."

With all the aplomb and assurance in the world I told him that by the time I was out of the army I would be able to walk.

"And when's that going to be?" he queried.

"Quite soon, I think," I told him. "I am due to go to Hounslow tomorrow, and they only send you there from the hospital if you are going to be discharged."

Whether that was true or not I simply did not know. Anyway, he then said all right, I'd better sing, which I did, choosing for my song "A Bachelor Gay" from his show *The Maid of the Mountains*. When I'd finished, he said nothing but picked up his hat, turned to Merlin Morgan, his musical director, who had been playing for me, and to my father, and suggested we all go for a drink.

On the way out through the stage door of the Prince's Theatre, where I had had the interview and audition, we met José Collins coming in to collect mail. Evett introduced my father and then me with—

"This is William Green, you may have heard of him—oh, and this is his son. He may be joining us shortly."

My heart leapt, though I did not quite know whether he was having a joke at my expense or not. But he wasn't, for as we were finishing our drink a little later he broached the subject again, telling me that I had better write him as soon as I was demobbed, and if I could manage to get about at all reasonably he would see if he could fit me in somewhere.

I flung my crutches away that night—and picked them up again the next morning. After all, I had to get to Hounslow—which I did the next day. There I was promptly arrested for being absent without leave. My luck held, though, for I had been posted to Clacton the day previously; all my papers had already gone, and in spite of the fact that at 10 A.M. I had been reduced to the ranks—I had been a lance corporal—I found myself in charge of a party of ten en route for Clacton, where I was very nearly placed under arrest again for being improperly dressed. I had removed my one stripe immediately I had received the sentence. I was told to "put it up again pronto," which I did. I believe I am the only N.C.O. in the British army to be reduced to the ranks while still retaining his chevron. I was in fact discharged as a lance corporal.

Once I had settled down at Clacton I devoted myself assiduously to learning how to walk without the aid of crutches, and gradually I was able to discard them in exchange for two sticks. A month after I arrived I was discharged, and the first thing I did on reaching home was to write Evett and assure him I could walk, but failed to add that I still required two sticks to do it. Two days later I had a letter from him telling me I could join the company of *The Southern Maid* at Nottingham in two weeks' time. When the stage manager saw me and I told him why I was there, he exploded, "My God!"

However, I watched the show from the front that night and the next, and on the Wednesday I went on the stage as a professional for the first time, in the chorus. And those chorus boys were about the best it will ever be my good fortune to meet. I could not walk without the aid of sticks or some support or other, so I would go on to the side of the stage with my sticks and stack them up against a piece of scenery, and then two of the boys would come either side of me, take my arms, and on we would go for all the world as if we were good pals strolling along arm in arm. If it was possible for me to sit down during any scene, they arranged it and were always at hand to help me off.

The tour lasted some eight weeks, during which time I was paid what was to me a fortune after the army—three pounds a week—and at the end of which I was able to walk—slowly, it's true—onto the stage without the aid of anything or anybody. So much for the doctors' verdict.

The tour over, I returned home. One thing I had learned during that tour was that if I wished to get anywhere in my chosen profession I would most certainly have to work extremely hard and learn, not only to walk properly, but to dance again. My father, too, considered that I should also begin to study voice production and elocution—with some considerable stress on the matter of diction.

To the latter end I entered for the vocal scholarship to the Royal College of Music—my father's old college (he had won a scholarship there). At about the same time I got to hear about the generosity of a grateful government, which was offering tuition fees and maintenance to ex-servicemen—a scheme that was known as the higher education of ex-officers and men of three services. I promptly made application for both the fees and the maintenance.

While waiting to sit for the preliminary examination for the scholarship, I went away with my sister and a friend to Bettws-y Coed in North Wales, where I spent the days when it wasn't raining walking the country lanes. Every day my leg grew stronger and stronger. But there was one thing I could not do. I could not put my weight on my leg when the knee was bent. I had no control below the knee. Consequently the effort of swinging the leg forward from the hip far enough to allow it to straighten and thus permit me to put my weight on it created a considerable limp. So on the days when it was raining I spent some hours in front of a full-length mirror practising swinging the leg while trying to eliminate the limp.

I sat for the preliminary scholarship examination very shortly after my return from Bettws-y Coed, and within a week was notified that I would be required to sit for the final in a few weeks' time. I practised hard during those few weeks, my father giving me lessons. The great day came and I went to London, and eventually sat for the final. My ordeal over, I was told to wait. About an hour later Claude Aveling, the registrar of the college, came out to me and said, "I believe you have an application for a government grant in respect of training at the Royal College?" I told him yes, I had.

"In that case," he went on, "would you mind forgoing the scholarship? Yes, you have won it, but there is another candidate very close to you. He, unfortunately—or fortunately, depending on how you look at it—has not the necessary qualifications to apply for government assistance, not having been in the army, navy, or air force. That was not his fault. If you will forgo the scholarship we can award it to him, and you will get the grant. I might point out that the scholarship is only worth £80 a year, plus tuition fees, whereas the grant is worth £130 plus fees." I accepted the grant. He could not tell me when the grant would come through, or when I would be notified that I was to commence my studies, so, as I had to live in the interim, I again wrote to Mr. Evett and once again found myself on tour, this time with *The Maid of the Mountains*.

We opened in Belfast, staying there for two weeks and then going on to Dublin for a further two weeks, where José Collins joined the cast for a special season. On the way down from Belfast to Dublin George Fearnley, an actor who was doubling the part of Antonio in the first act with Crumpet in Acts II and III, was taken ill with appendicitis and rushed off to the hospital as soon as we arrived. I was understudying one of the baritone parts, and also functioning as assistant stage manager, besides going on in the chorus. As we arrived in the theatre for the evening performance the stage manager instructed me to warn George D'Almaigne, a member of the chorus, that he was to go on for the part of Crumpet. I said very good, but what about Antonio? At that Drew nearly hit the ceiling.

"My God! We haven't got an understudy for the part, and George certainly can't go on for that, even if he knew it." (George was turned 70.)

"What are we going to do?" I asked.

"Heaven only knows," said Drew.

I thought for a minute, then decided to take the plunge—after all it was a chance. It wasn't a big part, only the first act, and not many lines, not more than two pages.

"I think I could learn it if I could have a book," I said rather nervously, and wishing to heaven I hadn't the moment I'd said it.

"I'll get you one right away. Get to your room and start making up. I'll bring the book to you and the wig and costume. Be on the stage at the quarter and I'll rehearse you."

Well, now the fat was in the fire. I would have to do it willy-nilly. And there were several jobs I still had to do as assistant stage manager, one of them being to warn the principals of the change of cast. When I told José Collins there would be a change as Fearnley was off and that D'Almaigne would be going on as Crumpet she repeated my question to Drew. Who would be playing Antonio? I very timidly told her I would.

Well, at least I can always say that I was once kissed by José Collins. And on stage she was charm itself, and though I did not have a great deal to do with her, in what little I had she helped me with a capital H. From that moment on I swore that if ever I should find myself in her position I too would give all the help I could. I know now that it is not for entirely un-selfish reasons that a principal will help an understudy. The more they help, the better will the understudy's performance be; the show will suffer less, and there will be no loss of credit to the principal in consequence. I have known principals who would give no help at all. For that there is no excuse. It is bad for the show, bad for them, unkind, and unworthy of any who call themselves actors.

"The show must go on." Well, this one did, and I'm glad to say that I didn't do too badly, thanks to all the assistance I received. There was one rather embarrassing moment, though. The one principal I had forgotten to warn of the change in cast was Leonard Mackay, who was the Baldasarre. Right towards the end of the act it was my job to rush onto the stage down a rather steep ramp—only in my case I made the entrance with a long step, a hop, and a final skid down the remainder of the ramp.

That in itself was sufficient to startle Mackay, but when I picked myself up and he saw an unfamiliar face and heard an unfamiliar voice crying "Baldasarre, Baldasarre, they've caught Teresa!" it was too much. The prompt book said: "Baldasarre takes Antonio by the shoulders as he says: 'Caught

Teresa! Who? What have they done with her?'" Not so
Leonard. He took me more or less by the throat, shook me
like a rat so that my cap and wig under it both fell off and said,
in a very audible stage whisper, "Who the hell are you?" I
managed to gasp out my name, and then we carried on with
the end of the act.

Some five weeks later in Glasgow, where we were booked
for a week but stayed three, if I remember rightly—though it
may have been four, due to the railway strike which kept us
marooned there—Eric Marshall, the actor I was understudying,
was off one night with a cold, and my chance came to go on for
him. Again everybody was most helpful, though the one place
they couldn't help me was in the first act when I started my
first song with the second verse—and nobody could remember
the words of the first. At the last minute they came to me,
though, and I managed to finish the song with it. Two weeks
after that my principal was called to London and my real
chance came. I was able to open on the Monday night and got
my first real notice in the following day's papers. Like everybody else, they were very kind.

Two weeks later I received instructions to report to the
Royal College of Music, and commence my studies, beginning
at the half-term. I handed in my notice and left the company
at Liverpool two weeks later. But before I left I went to Alderhey Hospital, enquired for the doctor who had sentenced me
to a life of crippledom, persuaded him to see me, and walked
into his office. I quote his words when he saw me:

"It's not true! It can't be! That man would never walk again.
Still—miracles do happen, or it just shows you what a bloody
fine doctor I am. Come and have a drink."

THREE

Audition

It was rather like going back to school. Or rather, it was like going to a new school, which of course it really was, only it was dignified by the name of college—and a royal college at that. We arrived—myself and several other students—and stood around in a little group, as new boys do. Whether there were any new girls I just don't know. If there were, then they were carefully segregated, as I didn't see any—any new ones, that is. I saw several girls, but they were obviously in their third year at least. They had that sort of supercilious look about them that has always denoted the senior at school. That pitying look that seems to say, "You'll soon learn." Later we were taken into the office, full particulars were taken, and eventually we were led into the director's office.

I knew Gustav Garcia was still on the professorial staff, in fact the number one of the singing professors, in spite of his age, which was in the neighborhood of eighty. Gustav Garcia was the son of Manoel Garcia, and Manoel Garcia had not only invented the laryngoscope (an instrument widely used today by throat specialists and dentists) but had taught the

41

Swedish Nightingale, Jenny Lind, to sing. He had also given my father some lessons, about four in all. He would not give him any more. "For" he said, "I am retiring." He was then about ninety-eight. But my father, not being able to go on with Manoel, had continued his studies with the son, Gustav.

Could I do anything other than carry out my studies under the man who taught my father? I thought not, and asked the director if I might be allotted to Signor Garcia. I was. And the following day I had my first lesson with him. But if I thought that being the son of my father would help me in any way, I soon learned different. Before I was halfway through my lesson (my individual lesson, for three students were in the studio at the same time with twenty minutes of individual tuition and forty of listening to the other two), he stopped me in the middle of a song and said:

"That is the last song you will sing for a year, maybe two. Your father—ah, he could sing. His voice was one an angel would envy. But you—you are not your father. Me—my father—magneeficent. Sing? He sing like all the angels—he teach Jenny Lind. Me? I am good. I have a great baritone voice (he had even at the age of eighty)—I teach your father. My son—pah. You? We start on exercises, and hope!"

God bless him (he died at the age of eighty-six), I never had a great voice, nor even a big one, but what little I have I have kept solely because Gustav Garcia taught me how to use it. And as for diction—nothing would satisfy him but perfection. I knew then why it was that one of my father's proud boasts was that nobody ever needed to read the words as he was singing them. Through life I have tried to emulate him and carry out Garcia's teachings in that respect, for as he himself would say, "What is the use of telling a story if no one can hear what it is all about?"

My extra subject was elocution, the professor for that subject being Cairns James. In years gone by he had appeared in many of the Gilbert and Sullivan operas, and had worked with Gilbert himself, his favorite roles being Jack Point and the Duke of Plaza Toro. But we never touched G. & S. at the Royal College. It was looked upon there as being rather lowbrow. Consequently I was not overly impressed when James showed me photos of himself in some of the parts. On one occasion one or two of the students at one of the full dramatic classes asked him if it would be possible to do one of the G. & S. operas. His reply was a sorrowful No. I then dropped a brick by asking, "What is Geeandess?"

My grant from the Government was for three years, and I don't think I could have spent three happier years anywhere in spite of the fact that I lost my father in April of 1920—just two days after my twenty-first birthday. I knew he was very ill when I left home on the Monday to return to college after the Easter vacation, but it still came as a blow when I received a telegram on the Tuesday to say he had died during the night. Tuesday was one of my days for singing, and I got the wire just after I had completed my hour. When I was able to recover my composure, I went back to Gustav Garcia to tell him that I would not be coming for my Thursday lesson and why. For a moment he sat stock still, then rose from his chair, took my hand in one of his, and placing the other round my shoulders kissed me on both cheeks. Then he led me to the door, swallowed hard and said, "Very well, my boy—I understand," closed the door, and presumably went on with his lessons. It was close on six months before he mentioned my father's name to me after that—and I was grateful. My father and I had been great friends.

Early in 1922 I was taking a stroll through Piccadilly one Saturday afternoon with the idea of eventually being very extravagant and having tea at Lyons Corner House, and maybe dinner a little later at one or another of the little restaurants in Soho—my favourite at the time being a very small place, "Le Diner Français"—when I ran across a fellow student, B. R. L. Smith, an organist and son of the Bishop of Knaresborough. He asked me what I was doing and would I like to go to the Prince's Theatre with him. With a bit of luck, and if we got there early enough, we could probably get a couple of standing-room places at the back of the circle for 3/6. I asked him what he was going to see, and he told me "The D'Oyly Carte Opera Company." I wasn't feeling very much like opera, I told him, but he insisted I would enjoy it, so I gave in. We had our dinner and then made our way to the Prince's. We were a little late in arriving and the curtain had already gone up on *The Gondoliers,* but we were allowed in as we were only standing at the back of the circle. As we went in two men were getting out of a gondola at the back of the stage. Obviously, thought I, these are the Gondoliers. They began to sing.

"Oh, good Lord," I thought, "it's in Italian."

However, I settled down to watch, and as the curtain came down on the first act agreed that it wasn't too bad. After a couple of drinks in the bar I went back for the second act feeling much brighter, and thoroughly enjoyed Derek Oldham's singing of "Sparkling Eyes." The funny thing was, I already knew the song. I had heard my father sing it. And it had once been sung at a college concert. I often wonder how the singer got away with it.

Not very long after Derek had finished his last encore, both Bernard Smith and I were very nearly thrown out of the theatre for creating a disturbance. I suppose in a way it was a disturbance, but it was in no way our fault. It was just that I had never in my life heard anything so funny as Leo Sheffield saying: "Because a Lord High Chancellor . . . should never . . . place himself in the position of being told to—er—tuck in his tuppenny . . ." and of course, I began to laugh. Patrons in the back row started shushing us, and eventually one of the ushers came to us and quietly informed us that "if you can't control yourselves, you'll have to leave the theatre."

That was my first introduction to both Gilbert and Sullivan, and Gilbert and Sullivan audiences. Both are something apart, and at the time I could not understand an audience that didn't want to laugh at something funny. I didn't realize that 99.9 per cent of them already knew it, and probably all the others, by heart and were quite prepared not only to shush me and my friend, but to prompt any one of the performers on the stage if he should fluff.

There is another type of patron—and that is the type who will sing every word and speak every line with the actor as the show proceeds. A story is told of one of this type who, seated in the third or fourth row of the stalls and singing and speaking with the performer in a voice sufficiently audible to be heard within a radius of three or four seats in all directions, was tapped on the shoulder by the gentleman behind, who whispered to him: "Would you mind speaking up, sir? I'm afraid they"—pointing up to the stage—"can't hear you up there."

When the curtain fell at the end we made our way out to the street, and there was no hesitation in my voice when I replied "Yes" to Bernard's question as to whether I would like to see another of the operas, and he suggested *The Yeomen of the Guard*.

We went the following week. Derek Oldham was the Fairfax, Nellie Briercliffe the Phoebe, Elsie Griffin the Elsie, Leo Sheffield the Shadbolt, and Henry Lytton the Jack Point. To say I was moved would be putting it mildly. I was intensely moved, and very impressed with Henry Lytton's performance of Point. As we left the theatre I said to Bernard: "What a part! What a performance! What wouldn't I give to play that part!"

"If you ever do," he said, "I'll come and see you in it." In Leeds, in 1932, he did.

I didn't complete my three years at college by approximately nine months. One day I was approached, through the good offices of the Chisholm sisters—Lena and Peggy, a violinist and a pianist respectively, who had also studied at the Royal College of Music. They had for some little time been doing a musical act "on the halls" and were at that moment with Herman Darewski in his act "Thirty Minutes of Melody." Would I join the act as the baritone? Arthur Argent was leaving the following week to go to South Africa and Herman wanted someone to replace him. He could offer me £8 per week. That did it. My fortune was made, said I to myself, said I. I accepted at once, and for four weeks sang "The Voice of the Sea Is Calling" and the "Floral Dance."

Then I had a row. Herman would make his entrance just as I finished the last note of the "Floral Dance" and steal my applause. I objected to this—hang it, he might have given me a moment to collect a little to myself—and gave in my notice.

But at least I can say that I—or at any rate, the act I was in—topped the bill at the Palladium before Danny Kaye.

Before I concluded my engagement with Herman—we parted very good friends, incidentally—I called once more at Daly's Theatre. Robert Evett had severed his connection with the George Edwardes Company by this time, so I wasn't too sure of my reception. Nevertheless, I walked out of Daly's with a contract in my pocket to play the part of Paul Petrov in a touring company of *Sybil*.

For the first time in my life I was going to have my name in print in front of the theatre. It was not until I saw it that I realised W. Martyn-Green was not quite the sort of name to use for billing. I did not want to use my father's name, even though it *was* mine as well, for fear people would think I was trying to trade on his name. It never dawned on me that those people who would know and remember his name would not be the sort of people I would be concerned with—a few maybe, but not the vast majority. So—William Green was out. That left only one thing for me, and before the tour came to an end I had cut out the hyphen and Martyn Green was born.

The tour ended in May, and I was out of work. I couldn't go back to college, as I had definitely terminated my grant; so I had to find work. I haunted agents' offices daily—but no one seemed to know me. They very soon did get to know me, but not in a way that would be likely to do me any good. However, one day I was seated in an agent's waiting room, making myself the sort of nuisance by which many other agents had got to know me, when a woman walked in, looked at me hard in passing, and went straight into the inner sanctum. Three minutes later I was in there myself being offered a job in a musical sketch. The woman was Haidee de Rance, a violinist.

My salary was five pounds—what a comedown! We had a one week's tryout booked for Guildford, I think it was, and we rehearsed for a week at a house in Brondesbury.

At one point in our sketch I had to register deep emotion while seated at the piano, the climax of which culminated in my collapsing and burying my head in my arms with a crash on the keyboard. I knew I was good in that bit. All through the rehearsals it was the bit I looked forward to, and I could hardly wait for the moment to arrive when I would do it in the actual performance. At last it came—my great dramatic moment. The audience could not help but be spellbound. With a terrific crash I came down on the keyboard. But before the last note of that horrible discord had faded away the audience was hysterical with laughter. We lasted the week, but only just— and once again I was out of work.

My next venture was as juvenile lead in what was pleased to be known as A Revue with a Story—*Shuffle Along*. It was while I was appearing at the Stoke Newington Empire with that show that I ran into an old college friend—Ethel Maclelland. I was in town for the day and met her in Bond Street. Naturally we stopped for a chat, and during the course of conversation I asked her what she was doing these days.

"Oh," she said airily, "I'm principal soprano with the D'Oyly Carte Opera Company." I think she went on to tell me that they were playing at Richmond or some such place. Suddenly she looked straight at me and said, "I think you'd do quite well in G. & S."

Now that was an idea that had never really struck me till that moment, so I promptly asked how to set about getting into it. She told me that I would have to write in and ask for an audition, and when they were holding one they would send for me. I was only in town for the day, after which my Revue with a Story was due to go up to Hull and generally wander around in the north of England for some weeks; so instead of writing I went straight to the Savoy Hotel, where the D'Oyly Carte Company had their offices, and asked to see Mr. Carte.

I was ushered into an office. Behind a desk sat a woman to whom my usher said: "This gentleman would like to see Mr. Carte." Then to her question I answered, "No, I have no appointment. I wanted to see him about an audition."

"If you want an audition," she told me, "you will have to write in for one"—and there was some degree of finality in her voice.

"I'm afraid that if Mr. Carte wants to hear me sing," for all the world as if I were doing him a great favour, "he will have to hear me today, as I am only in town until 4:30 and will not be returning for some time." A look of complete incredulity came over her face. "Of course," I went on, "if Mr. Carte likes he can come down to Stoke Newington and see me work any night this week—first or second house. If he would let me know I will arrange for seats. I'll send two along in any case."

Without saying a word she rose rather dazedly from her seat, and walked out of her office. In about five minutes she returned, the incredulous look even more evident than before. Seating herself once more behind her desk, she looked at me, her mouth open, and then more or less gasped out: "Mr. Carte will see and hear you at three o'clock this afternoon. I suppose you have some music?" I nodded. "I don't suppose you have an accompanist with you?" I shook my head. "We'll find one for you. Be here at ten minutes to three sharp. Ask for me—I'm Miss Dawe, Mr. Carte's secretary." As I left her office she was leaning back in her desk chair muttering: "Well! Well! I don't know—I really don't—"

Promptly at 2:50 I was in that office. My eagerness, I now confess, was not so much that I was keen on doing Gilbert and Sullivan as the fact that I had been told it was a pretty certain forty-eight weeks of work per year, and that meant something to me, as the show I was then with was booking up dates more or less week by week as we went along. Arriving at the office, I was greeted by Miss Dawe, who had by this time recovered her poise and was inclined to treat the whole affair philosophically. She introduced Miss Evans, who was to accompany me. I chose a song called "Mother Carey," which is a pretty quick-fire number, and I chose it because I had been warned by Ethel Maclelland that diction was an important thing with Carte.

After a quick scan-through with Miss Evans I was led into what was known as the "White Room," one of the large banqueting rooms of the Savoy Hotel overlooking the Embankment. Mr. Carte came in two or three minutes after—punctually on the dot of three, I noticed—and I was introduced. He sat down, and I sang. He then had a few words with me, and asked me what I was doing at the time. I told him, and repeated the offer of tickets to him.

"Yes, y-e-s," he said, stroking his chin, a habit I seem to recollect in him when he was amused. "Yes, that might be quite nice. Stoke Newington, I think you said. Y-e-s," and with that he got up and walked out. I gathered up my music, and then Miss Dawe went on: "Perhaps you could leave an itinerary, or an address where we can reach you during the next few weeks?" The old story, thought I, but—well, perhaps these people do mean it—so I returned with her to the office and complied.

F O U R

Joining D'Oyly Carte

Whether Carte ever used the tickets I sent, or whether he sent Richard Collett, or even whether they were used at all, I never found out. I didn't care to ask Freddie Turner, the owner of *Shuffle Along*, as at that time I naturally didn't want him to know that I had been singing to another firm while still in his show. Approximately four weeks later the revue was playing at Aldershot, and I received a letter from Carte requesting me to learn Lord Mountararat's song, "When Britain really ruled the waves," together with the dialogue with Lord Tolloller from the scene following the song, and would I please attend the Savoy Theatre on such and such a date for a further audition? From Aldershot I could very easily get up to town.

Arriving at the Savoy, I met a genial, white-haired, patriarchal-looking gentleman. There were a number of other candidates for audition and he greeted every one of us, asking our names—which he duly ticked off on a large sheet of foolscap—and telling us his own—J. M. Gordon. He also informed me that he would be speaking Tolloller's lines in the dialogue, and that I wasn't to worry, everything would be all right. Then he took another look at me, took off a pair of spectacles, replaced them with another, and said: "Ah, yes, you're the young man who is touring with—ah—a musical—ah—ahem, yes. Well, as I said, don't worry—er—too much."

I came to know that great gentleman very well in the years that followed, but I must admit that remark of his turned my feet to lead, my heart and liver to a jelly, and my tonsils to ten times their normal size. At the same time I had my first— though it was only the first—view of the one remaining true link with Gilbert himself, and incidentally a great actor. During that audition he not only spoke Tolloller's lines to my Mountararat's (which I regret to say I spoke so badly that I will never know quite why I was eventually offered a contract) but also Yum-Yum's to an aspiring Nanki-Poo; Pooh-Bah's to a would-be Ko-Ko; the Duchess of Plaza-Toro's to hopeful Dukes; Fairfax's to budding Elsies; and the Fairy Queen's to enthusiastic Iolanthes. And not once did he look at a book.

J. M. Gordon—Jimmy Gordon generally to all and sundry, though Jimmy was not his name—was the stage director and producer to both the D'Oyly Carte Companies that were in existence at that time: the Repertory Company, the cast of which included Henry Lytton, Bertha Lewis, Leo Sheffield, Derek Oldham, Darrell Fancourt, Elsie Griffin, Winifred Lawson, and Joseph Griffin (no relation to Elsie), and carried the full repertoire of operas, with the exception of *The Sorcerer, Utopia, Ltd.*, and *The Grand Duke;* and the Small Company with Frank Steward, Winifred Williamson, Hilton Leyland, Ethel Maclelland, Charles Goulding, Margaret Philo, William Thompson, and, up to a few weeks before I went with Herman Darweski and his "Thirty Minutes of Melody," Arthur Argent, whose place I had filled in that act.

Jimmy Gordon had in the past appeared in several of the operas, had been directed by W. S. Gilbert himself, and had been coached by, and had sung under the baton of Arthur S. Sullivan. The link was direct. What parts he played, other than that of the Colonel in *Patience*, I'm afraid I don't know. He never spoke of any other. But his knowledge of the operas and of Gilbert's method of production was tremendous. It was said of him that he had forgotten more than all the others put together had ever remembered—and I can quite believe it. His stories of both Gilbert and Sullivan were legion, and were always entertaining or instructive—or both.

I remember him once having some difficulty in getting one of the newer principals to speak one line in the way he wished it, and the way in which he insisted Gilbert intended it. Patiently he went over and over the line—a very short line, giving the inflections he wanted, and over and over again the principal in question kept saying it the way he himself wanted it. At last Jimmy said: "Mr. So-and-so, there is, I am afraid, only one way in which that line may be said, only one way. Let me explain. It is not the first time that a performer has wanted to speak a line his own way. It happened in Sir William's time. As Sir William himself pointed out, that one line represents one-half page of writing. You cannot fool about with it!"

Yes, he was a very great man, and when he died during the Second World War, the D'Oyly Carte Opera Company lost something they will never be able to replace. They lost someone who had not only the knowledge, but the ability to impart that knowledge. At times he was a martinet and would brook no interference or deviation from the set routine. I have much to be grateful for where he is concerned. He spent hours coaching me in every part I played.

Every night he would stand at the back of the auditorium, where, with a large stenographic notebook in his hand, he would follow every movement on the stage, at the same time making notes in his own peculiar method of shorthand. Every night, after the curtain had come down, he would call rehearsals for the next morning. Sometimes just one or two of the principals—even Henry Lytton was not entirely free—and sometimes the full company. Then he would repair to his rooms and after a light supper of cheese, crackers, and a glass of whisky, sit down and—in his own words—"transcribe his notes." The following morning he would turn up at the rehearsal with sheaves of notes, all written out in "good clerkly script" and proceed with a full morning's rehearsing. At the end he was quite likely to hand you any of the notes that might concern you personally, just to keep them in your mind.

At times he would find himself in a theatre where the lighting at the back of the auditorium was not at all good, and in one case the only illumination he had by which to write his notes came from an old-fashioned gas bracket. I don't think it was entirely the gas bracket's fault, as he was frequently known to scribble his notes while still watching the stage. But the following morning's rehearsal had to be cancelled. It had been called for eleven o'clock, and was for the full company. J.M.G., as he was sometimes called, arrived late, an unprecedented thing in itself. After greeting us all with his usual bright and cheery "Good morning, ladies and gentlemen," he suddenly grew very red in the face, stuttered a bit, and then said: "I'm sorry, everybody, but I'm afraid I will have to cancel the rehearsal. I—er—well, the truth is, I—er—ah—cannot read the notes I took last night." And promptly burst into fits of laughter.

He has been credited with many *faux pas*—though some people may prefer to call the majority of them bons mots. At any rate, *faux pas*, bons mots, or just plain "gags," they were all extremely amusing, and all were given, made, or cracked during the course of the rehearsal then in progress. One of his most famous, which in a confidential moment he admitted he had once heard Gilbert crack, occurred during a rehearsal of *Princess Ida*. The chorus at one point in the first act are singing the words:

> You'll remain as hostage here;
> Should Hilarion disappear,
> We will hang you, never fear,
> Most politely,
> Most politely,
> Most—po—litely.

On the last line the ladies of the chorus curtsey, but they did not go down at the moment Gordon wanted them to. After one or two attempts he stopped the rehearsal and said: "No, ladies, no. You're doing it wrong. You must go *down* on the 'po,' not 'litely.' Now, shall we try it?" Crude? Maybe. Nevertheless, we thought it funny, and it was certainly effective.

My audition at the Savoy over, I informed the powers that be of the D'Oyly Carte Company that I would very likely be free in the autumn, and departed for Aldershot and *Shuffle Along*.

On the Saturday morning something, I know not what, prompted me to write a letter to Freddie Turner, the owner of the show, giving him a fortnight's notice. This written, I sealed it, placed it in my pocket, and when the appropriate time came, went to the theatre and carried on with the first house performance. As the curtain came down on that house I returned to my dressing room and proceeded to change into the requisite costume for the opening for the second house.

Shortly after there was a knock at my door and Freddie walked in with an envelope in his hand. Without saying a word I reached into my pocket, pulled out the letter I had written, and handed it to him as I accepted the one he held out to me. He smiled, I smiled—and put the letter in my pocket. Both of us knew what was in the other's letter—and neither of us opened the one we had. To this day I do not know whether I was sacked or he accepted my notice, and some twenty-three or twenty-four years later, when we were playing golf together, he admitted that he was never certain himself. He knew I had been for auditions to the D'Oyly Carte and that was why he had decided to give me notice, and I'm bound to admit that I've often wondered how he found out. He certainly would not tell me even after all those years.

During that two weeks a newcomer to the cast arrived as a replacement for one of the company who had been unavoidably detained a couple of weeks or so previously and who was at the time I left a guest of His Majesty at one of the larger of his supervised retreats. I cannot say that I met the newcomer other than to say a brief "Good morning" or "Good evening" as I entered or left the theatre. He was busy with rehearsals, and as I was leaving and he was not going to appear until after I had left there was no call for us to work or rehearse together. Some years later we did meet, and many are the rehearsals we have attended together. He was Richard Walker, the man who eventually succeeded Sydney Granville in the Pooh-Bah or Fred Billington roles in the G. & S. operas.

Before I said farewell to *Shuffle Along* I took the opportunity to write to Mr. Carte and inform him that I would be free to consider a contract earlier than I had expected. In just over a week's time, to be exact. His reply was a request to attend at his office on the Monday I returned to town, which I did, walking out of the place with a contract in my pocket wherein I undertook to "sing, act, perform, and understudy during the run of the tour ending on or about the 25th of May, 1923, at a salary of six pounds per week." Two weeks later, I joined the Small Company at Northampton.

Rupert D'Oyly Carte was a strange man in many ways. A hardheaded businessman—I nearly said a hard businessman; extremely shy of meeting people and in consequence not very easy to converse with until one knew him well. He had a reputation for being rather mean and tight-fisted—a reputation not entirely deserved, for he was also shy of ever appearing charitable, and therefore his charitable and generous actions were nearly always carried out sub rosa. Seldom would he commit himself to a definite statement, particularly in business, but if he did no contract was ever needed, though one always had one. His word was his bond. Many's the time I have asked him for some clause to be included in my contract, and ninety-nine times out of a hundred his reply would be "I'll see," or "I'll make a note." Sometimes he would then let me know that he agreed, or that he did not, and sometimes he would just ignore the whole thing. But if by chance he had said to me at the time of asking, "I will do that," then I knew it would be done. There was no need for him to write and confirm.

I must confess that I was a little disappointed at being posted, as it were, to the Small Company, but the die was cast. I had signed my contract, so, as needs must when the devil drives, I went where I was sent. There was one crumb of comfort:

my contract was what Mr. Carte was pleased to term a "special" contract, and there in one corner was typed the word itself. What he meant by "Special" was that I got two pounds a week more than a chorister and was expected to play small parts. What he didn't tell me was that the majority of the chorus were on more or less the same sort of contract. But I had at least gone to Northampton with the express purpose of learning and rehearsing one part, and the first thing I ever did with them was to play—or, to quote Hilton Leyland, who was the Don Alhambra, go on for—the part of Luiz in *The Gondoliers*, with Mabel (Bill) Sykes as the Casilda, Frank Steward as the Duke of Plaza-Toro, and Winifred Williamson as his Duchess.

I continued to play—or go on for—the part for the rest of that tour. It was during the following tour that our stage manager, R. A. Swinhoe, took me on one side saying he didn't quite know what to do with me. He had to fit me in as an understudy some way or another. (By this time I, at my own request, as I thought, was going on in the chorus. Had I but known it, that was the firm's intention anyway. I had merely anticipated their intention). My voice, he told me, was too light for the baritone roles, the compass too low for the tenor roles. Did I think I could do anything with Jack Point? Jack Point! Could I! I modestly said I thought I might; so, giving me a libretto, he told me to look at the first act overnight and be at rehearsal the following day at eleven o'clock.

By the next morning I was practically word-perfect. This so impressed Swinny that he said: "Well, if you can do as well with the second act by tomorrow we'll have you ready for a rehearsal with Mr. Gordon when he arrives next week." J.M.G.

arrived the following Monday—it was his routine to spend approximately two weeks with the Repertory Company and two weeks with the Small Company alternately—and I had my first rehearsal of Point with him. Of course, I had already had several with him before, both individual, as when preparing for Luiz, and collective when he called the full company or full chorus.

Following that rehearsal I was appointed third understudy to Frank Steward, and began to study his parts in the other three operas the company was carrying for that tour. These, if my memory serves me aright, were *The Gondoliers, Iolanthe,* and of course *The Mikado;* the parts being the Duke, the Lord Chancellor, and Ko-Ko. J. Ivan Menzies was the first understudy, and towards the end of the tour he gave a trial performance of Jack Point, shortly after which he was transferred to the Repertory Company. What happened to the second understudy I never found out—I don't think I ever knew who it was—but on Menzies' departure for the Repertory Company, I was promoted to first understudy.

The unkind cut that went with that was that Luiz was taken from me and I was given the part of Antonio instead. That was explained to me by telling me that it would mean too many changes of cast if Frank Steward were ever off and I had to go on for him. It would necessitate someone going on for me as Luiz, whereas Antonio didn't matter so much. I accepted their explanation and the situation then, but later, when I was transferred to the Repertory as Lytton's understudy, the fact that I was again entrusted with Luiz did not seem to stack up with that explanation.

I eventually "went on for" and continued to play several

other parts, including Pish-Tush (*The Mikado*), Counsel (*Trial by Jury*), and Cox (*Cox and Box*, which is *not* Gilbert and Sullivan, but Sullivan and Burnand).

Which recalls to my mind a slightly awkward, but nevertheless amusing stage wait. It was when I was playing Cox in the Small Company. Bernard Manning was the Sgt. Bouncer; Reginald Burston, since known for his radio performances and as the musical director of several Drury Lane successes, including *Carousel*, was conducting. We had just reached the point where Bouncer has said a hurried "Yes, sir, good morning" and Cox seizes him by the wrist. At that precise moment the first notes of the introduction to a duet should be heard and Bouncer and Cox, in an exaggerated dramatic manner, take four steps downstage—but—there was no music. I looked at Bernard, he looked at me—and we did it again. And again— no music. By this time we were very nearly over the footlights. We both looked down to catch Reggie's eye—and we both failed.

We were not quite certain whether he was telling the leader a funny story, or helping him to find his place, but he was most certainly engrossed to the exclusion of all else in conversation with that gentleman. Bernard Manning, of course, did the only thing possible. He snapped his fingers and muttered a very audible "Pst! Pst! Reggie—stay Bouncer, stay." Reggie looked up, smiled, said "Eh? Oh—yes, of course." Leisurely he picked up his baton, tapped on the stand, and proceeded with the introduction. By which time the audience were in hysterics, and the first two or three lines of the duet went unheard.

I hope Reggie will forgive me for telling that story—also this one. He had a very beautiful but very definitely "one-man" chow dog which he occasionally brought to the theatre and left in the band room. One evening, during a performance of *Ruddigore*, he had returned to the pit for the second act, leaving the dog, as usual, in the band room. But someone either left the door open, or opened it not very long after the curtain had gone up, and the chow quite naturally took advantage of the fact and went to look for his master.

How he knew in what position Reggie worked in the theatre I do not know, but that he did there is no doubt, and not being able to find his way through the pass-door, the understage door to the orchestra pit, he made his way onto the stage and down to the footlights, and there wagged his tail at his master, just as the ancestors, having descended from their frames, were about to begin singing the "Coward, poltroon, etc. . . ." part of the choral introduction to the ghost scene. One of the ghosts, Harry Lambourne I believe his name was, realizing that something ought to be done, stepped out of the line and went to the animal with the intention of leading it gently and quietly off the stage. Harry Lambourne retired hurt!

Hurriedly handing his baton over to the leader, Reggie dashed from the pit, up onto the stage and into the wings, where he whistled to the dog, called him, practically shouted at him, all to no avail. The dog couldn't hear him with all that noisy singing going on, and besides, his master had disappeared through a hole right underneath his feet, and he wasn't going to move until he returned. So enter Reggie Burston, looking a rather incongruous figure in his white tie and tails among all those ancestors in their cavalier, Napoleonic, Nelsonian, Cromwellian, etc., dress. But the chow knew him and suffered himself to be quietly led off the stage. During the whole of this episode the cast carried on in noble fashion—and beyond an initial titter as the chow made his entrance, the audience remained quiet. To them—full marks!

Time went on, and I gradually became more confident in my work, and incidentally more and more fond of it. I worked hard: I rehearsed one or another of the parts practically every morning, and was on in the chorus, or playing one of the small parts, every evening. And then one day I had a letter from the office, signed by R. D'Oyly Carte, saying that he wished me to give a "trial performance" of Jack Point at the Theatre Royal, Bolton. I could hardly believe my eyes. My wish was about to come true. If I had known where Bernard Smith was at that moment I would have sent him a ticket.

Two days before I was due to go on I took the most frightful cold, and my voice very nearly left me. I was frantic. My mother had come up especially from London to see me play and worked like a slave over me. By the morning of "The Day" the cold was under control, but it had left me with a frightful sinus condition. But I wouldn't give in. At the full rehearsal that morning I must have sounded like a very ancient, weak, and asthmatic sparrow. But I persevered. Nothing was going to prevent me from going on that night but sudden death.

The curtain rose. Margaret Philo began her opening song. I was ready and waiting. Came my cue for entrance. I tried to speak, but couldn't—I would have given anything in the world to be able to turn tail and flee. But I couldn't. Two of the chorus girls seized my wrists, as they had done many times at rehearsals, the music for Jack Point's and Elsie Maynard's entrance began, the murmur of voices rose—and I was dragged onto the stage. There was nothing for it—I had to carry on willy-nilly. Suddenly I found myself speaking. Or was it I who was speaking? I didn't know. Yes, I did, though. It was Jack Point who was speaking—and very soon he was singing—and his voice didn't sound too bad.

At last it was over. Elsie had found her true love, and Jack had duly died of a broken heart. I had played my first Jack Point. I removed the tears from his eyes, restored his complexion to normal, and went back to my uncle's house, where I rejoined my mother and paternal relations, and, I am afraid, got a little tight.

That was in the early part of 1925. At the end of that tour, the last week in fact, we were playing at Westcliffe-on-Sea. I had some weeks before been informed that I would not be going on vacation with the rest of the company, but would be going over to the Repertory Company as "walking understudy" to Henry Lytton. Ivan Menzies, the then understudy, would be going on vacation and then taking over the "Lytton parts," as they were then becoming known, from Frank Steward, who had not been in very good health for a while and was retiring.

We opened at Westcliffe with *The Mikado*, and as usual I was in the chorus. The curtain had gone up on the second act; "Here's a how-de-do" was just coming to an end as I made my way onto the stage ready for the chorus entrance heralding the entrance of the Mikado himself, played by Bernard Manning. Frank danced off the stage, not, I thought to myself, looking particularly well, which he certainly wasn't. As he approached me, he took off his over-robe and pushed it into my hands, pointed to his throat, and collapsed in the stage manager's arms.

Frank did not appear again that week. That, in fact, was his last performance with the D'Oyly Carte for some years. I, of course, had to go on right away without any change of costume, make-up, or announcement. The effect on the audience can be well imagined. Rupert D'Oyly Carte came down to see each of the succeeding performances but, I am afraid, never once came round either to tell me whether I was good, bad, or indifferent, to wish me luck, or to kick me in the pants. However, I had at least had a little experience of playing some of the parts —in fact: Ko-Ko, the Duke of Plaza-Toro, the Lord Chancellor, Sir Joseph Porter, and the Judge in the curtain-raiser *Trial by Jury*.

The week completed, I packed my make-up in the theatre and my truck at my digs, and on the Sunday proceeded to Birmingham, where I joined the Repertory Company and once again met some old friends from the Small Company, including Charles Goulding, who had joined them some months previously.

In passing, it was following a Monday evening's performance of *The Mikado* in which I was playing the role of Pish-Tush that I received what I shall always consider to be one of my best notices. The local evening paper the following day said: ". . . Martyn Green as Margaret Philo made a winsome Yum-Yum. . . ." Margaret actually appeared in that performance as Pitti-Sing.

F I V E

The Repertory Company

I reported at the Prince of Wales Theatre, since utterly de-
stroyed by a bomb during the war, on the Monday morning
and asked for Frederick Hobbs, the stage manager.

On leaving the army I had had to go to an oculist, as I had
been experiencing some slight trouble with my left eye, primarily caused by a touch of mustard gas and aggravated by
a blow on the eye which left me with slightly blurred vision.
He prescribed a monocle for me, particularly for close work.
I was wearing it when Hobbs appeared—also wearing one.
Nothing was said other than to give me a welcome and take me
off to the front of the house and the manager's office, where
I was introduced to the company's business manager, C. C.
Pool—a rotund and genial-looking gentleman. He, too, was
wearing a monocle! Again nothing was said other than to welcome me, raise his eyebrows a trifle—at which his glass fell out
on its cord—and glance quizzically at Hobbs, who quietly removed his glass from his eye and handed me over officially to
him.

I took my cue, and removed mine from my eye as Hobbs
turned to leave the office. I followed him out, and we returned

to the stage and dressing rooms, where he pointed out to me the room I would be using. That done, he gave me a few instructions regarding the work I was expected to do and told me to report to him for rehearsal instructions that evening. He then took me down to the stage level. As we approached it a gentleman came out of the No. 1 room, and I was introduced to Henry Lytton. I was extremely glad that I had picked up my cue in the manager's office and removed the monocle. Henry was also wearing one!

As time went on my monocle was accepted—no remarks were made, no quizzical glances exchanged. But no one could blame them in the first instance for thinking, as they must have done, that I was perhaps indulging in a somewhat ill-timed joke—and one in not particularly good taste.

For the next twelve months, with the exception of the usual four to five weeks' vacation which I took some four weeks after joining with the remainder of the company, I toured the larger provincial cities and towns. Then came my first London season—three months at the Prince's Theatre.

It was this year that some sweeping changes were made. In the first place, *The Mikado* was redesigned and redressed. R.D.C. commissioned Arthur Ricketts for the job. All the old traditional costumes were scrapped. The bright and colourful scenery was replaced by a drab green, relieved only by a touch or two of an equally drab red, and in the second act by a backcloth depicting an impossible bridge spanning an equally impossible stream that appeared to run uphill. The bright and varicoloured robes of the male chorus were replaced by baggy trousers that looked not unlike oversize plus fours reaching down to the ankle, in a series of dull browns and greens, topped off with coolie hats, intermingled with a hat reminiscent of a question mark. Ko-Ko was put into a jet-black coat and diagonally striped oversize plus fours; Pooh-Bah into canary yellow; the Mikado's gorgeous black and gold became white, and Katisha's brilliant red an over-heavy white, from which she changed later into a dull green and old gold. The chorus ladies and the three little maids were treated a little better, but they lost their fans, and their attractive wigs were replaced by ones that terminated in a sort of flat pigtail. Nanki-Poo's first entrance was made wearing what was once described as "a rather tatty-looking dressing gown."

"But use is everything, and you come in time to like it." It can easily be imagined, though, that its reception was very mixed —both in the theatre on the opening night and in morning and evening papers the following day. Ricketts defended himself, and was backed up by R.D.C., by pointing out that the costumes worn up to that time were not correct, and Gilbert had only agreed to their use because it was impossible to get anything else ready in time. The ones he himself had designed, said Ricketts, were based upon authentic twelfth-century Japanese paintings.

Ricketts also redesigned and redressed *The Gondoliers* during the Savoy season of 1929. In this case it was received, if not with enthusiasm by the purists, at least without very much adverse criticism. The main objection was to the backcloth, where again he had given the impression that the Grand Canal ran uphill. One other opera was redesigned—*Patience*—but this was by Sheringham, and was so successful that it passed without comment.

The 1926 Prince's Theatre season was the first season Dr. Malcolm Sargent was associated with the company. Here he took over the chair from Harry Norris. It was this overriding that eventually led to Norris's resigning from the company.

My first contact with Dr. Sargent came when rehearsals started for *The Gondoliers*. As usual, everyone was called for a piano rehearsal with Malcolm first. I was down to sing and dance the role of Antonio—a small part with but one number, "The merriest fellows are we." The full chorus was called at the same time. Reaching the point where Antonio begins to sing his solo—there are two to three bars of introductory music and Antonio does a very quick little dance step, as he does at the end of each of the first two lines and again in between the two verses—I realised that Malcolm was taking it at a smuch slower tempo than I was used to, or at which I could both sing and dance it. I stopped singing; Malcolm stopped playing and asked me what was the matter. I explained and was promptly told that I knew nothing about it. That was the tempo he was setting and that was the tempo at which it would be taken. I pointed out that it was impossible to dance it at that speed. There was a law of gravity that said when you went up you had to come down and that the law of gravity wasn't going to take much notice of any tempo other than the one set by itself.

Naturally, Sargent was a little annoyed. But so was I when he insisted on his tempo, and after a little further argument it was decided to leave it for the time being—that meant until he took the final rehearsal with full orchestra the morning of the opening performance.

Came that morning and once again "The merriest fellows are we"—and the same tempo. At this rehearsal our own Harry Norris was present, also J. M. Gordon. Both were inclined to be on my side, and both came to me later—after the inevitable argument with Sargent, my argument with him, not theirs, though they had both suggested to him that a little elasticity on his part would be a good thing—and suggested to me that perhaps if I went to him during the "break" and had a quiet word with him it might do some good. So I did that, but he was adamant—finishing his argument with "In any case, if you take it at the speed you want, the audience will never hear the words —not yours," he went on hurriedly, seeing I was just about to explode, "but the chorus words."

"Oh, really!" I said with all the sarcasm I could put into my voice, "And do you know what the chorus words are?"

"No—I can't remember them just at the moment," he replied.

"Well, I'll tell you," I said, "They are 'Tra la la la.'"

We compromised on the tempo.

Later on we did *Cox and Box* together, and I'm glad to say that our relations were completely harmonious.

Apart from the natural excitement of a London season there was during the whole of that 1926 season a subdued excitement, due to the fact that just one week after it closed in early December the company was due to embark for Canada on its first coast-to-coast tour. We were due to sail from Liverpool on the S.S. *Metagama*—a Canadian Pacific liner—on December 24th, the last performance at the Prince's being on the eighteenth.

For the majority of us it was our first ocean trip, and we intended to make the most of it. It might almost be said that the festivities began with the company's arrival at Euston for the boat train. It was undoubtedly one of the most boisterous rail journeys that I have ever been on. In those days leaving for a tour abroad was a simple matter. You could take what you wanted with you, and as much money as you wished. Not as on my last two trips, when I had to get export licences for every piece of jewelry over and above a watch and a signet ring; declare the amount of sterling I carried, and carry a sheaf of documents proving I had been vaccinated, chlorinated, arbitrated; go through customs, etc. No, we just showed our passports and steamer tickets and went on board.

Christmas Day, our first full day at sea, found us somewhere off the coast of Northern Ireland. It was a perfect day. The sea was calm, and the sun was warm enough for a spring day. Everyone was about, taking the sun, being initiated into the mysteries of shuffleboard, deck tennis, and the variety of deck games that a ship has to offer. Around about eleven o'clock in the morning all the children of the ship were brought up to the main lounge, where there was a huge Christmas tree, laden with presents for them. The ship was not full, by any means, there being only eighty-odd cabin passengers, of which the D'Oyly Carte Opera Company made some fifty or more. Second class and steerage were about as full in proportion, but to everyone's intense dismay the number of children aboard had been misjudged, and it turned out that quite a few of them got no presents. Hard lines, but there was little that could be done.

The day progressed. Pre-luncheon cocktails were taken, and everyone was down for lunch. Games or after-luncheon naps in one's deck chair were indulged in as your fancy took you. Came tea, and that strangely quiet hour that descends upon every ship just before one goes below to dress for dinner. I was seated alongside Doris Hemingway, now Mrs. Harry Norris, on the promenade deck. Farther along the deck Charles Goulding was to be seen with closed eyes quietly z-z-z-ing away. Doris and I started to sing some carols. Quite quietly.

Then I had an idea that it would be fun to go and annoy Charles by singing them to him. It was impossible, we just could not make him even open one eye, so we left to seek fresh fields and pastures new.

We eventually made our way into the drawing room, where a few odd couples were indulging in mild flirtations. We began to annoy them and succeeded beyond our wildest expectations. They even threw money at us. Well, that started something. Doris said something about "kids and presents"; one of the couples rose from their settee saying, "We're in on that"; and for the next three-quarters of an hour we toured the ship, picking up recruits as we went along, not to mention the money. We were dragged down to the engine room, where we sang to the engineers; to the galleys, where we sang to the chefs; to the officers' quarters, where we sang to the officers off watch. And we finished up in the purser's cabin, handing over to him a sum of money, I forget the exact amount, but sufficient to buy all the kids a couple of presents apiece and still leave something to hand over to the seamen's charities. It was a grand Christmas Day.

We landed at St. John, N.B., on Sunday, January 2, 1927, in a temperature bordering on zero, and by noon of the same day had commenced our journey by rail to Montreal, which we reached the following morning at about eight o'clock.

Shortly after we left St. John I went into the dining car for some lunch. By this time, that is to say after some nine days aboard, the state of my personal exchequer was not quite as healthy as one would have liked. My first salary would not be paid to me until the next Friday. A strict economy seemed to be indicated. I would study the menu and select something that would give me the most food for the least money. To describe that menu would fill two or three chapters, so I won't attempt it, but after approximately half an hour's reading I selected a "Small steak. $1. The price of the main item includes choice of vegetables, roll, butter, and coffee."

By the time I had made my selection I had been joined at the table by three other male travellers unconnected with the company and obviously natives of the country. The waiter took my order and looked enquiringly at the other three. All three said they would wait a while and look over the menu. While waiting for my order to arrive I glanced at some of the literature provided by a thoughtful railroad company, while the other three chatted quietly among themselves. It did not strike me at the moment that they were not looking at the menu.

My meal arrived: an oval serving dish with a steak on it fully two inches thick and overlapping the ends of the dish by two or three inches at each end. I looked at the waiter and said; "But I ordered a 'small' steak."

"That's right," he told me, "that's a small steak." I studied it for a moment and then asked him, for heaven's sake, what would I have got if I'd ordered a large one.

"There ain't no large ones," he said. Then he turned to the other three and asked them for their orders.

"Just bring three more hot plates and three orders of vegetables," said one. "We'll join this gentleman in his steak." The waiter went off, and the speaker turned to me. "Stranger here?" he asked. I nodded, and told him I had arrived on the *Metagama* that morning. "Thought so," he went on. "Mind if we help you with your steak? Take a tip from me, only order 'small' steaks between three or more. That's why, when we heard you order, we didn't bother. Thought we might be able to join you."

It was an excellent steak and served the four of us amply

and well. What was more, my exchequer benefited to the extent of 60 cents, the meal costing me but a quarter of the steak plus 10 cents for vegetables, which had, of course, become an extra, and a 5-cent tip.

Not long after I had settled down in my hotel, I received an invitation to go to an ice hockey game, which I accepted, went to, and was duly thrilled and horrified. The only surprising thing about that game to me was that none of the players left their brains behind them on the ice, and that all appeared to be quite good friends once they were off the ice. I had been a little surprised to see the players come onto the rink in the first instance padded to such an extent that I wondered how they could move. Before the first period was halfway through I understood.

The game over, we all went along to our host's house. Our host was an Englishman, a very brilliant surgeon, Sir Henry Gray, an old friend of the company's back in England in the days when he had been practising there. Rupert Carte, who had crossed over to New York before us, taking in the Winthrop Ames production of *Iolanthe* en route for Montreal, was also at the house. Sir Henry was giving this party as a sort of good luck and a rousing welcome to us. We reached his place about 11 P.M. Carte sat in a far corner of the room and spoke to nobody if he could help it, and then only in monosyllables, until about 11:45, when he rose and said: "I think it's time everybody went home." One voice was raised in protest, that of Sir Henry Gray—but we went home. All of us.

✳✳✳✳✳✳✳✳✳✳✳✳✳✳✳✳✳✳✳✳✳✳✳✳

S I X

First Canadian Tour

Our reception at our opening the following night was most enthusiastic (we opened with *The Gondoliers*). The following morning's papers were eulogistic, and the remainder of our stay was a matter of "House Full" boards every night.

Our main trouble was to judge our laughs. Though quite a large proportion of them came in the same places as at home in England, there were many places where a laugh was expected, but did not come, and where we did not expect them and were caught on the wrong foot, as it were, because one came. One place in particular Leo Sheffield found very disconcerting. Following on the famed "Cachucha" chorus and dance, Leo as the Don Alhambra discovers a "common little drummer boy" whom he takes by the ear and leads off. As he returns to the two kings the little boy runs after him and thumbs his nose at him. At home here in England that is always good for a big laugh. There in Canada it was recieved either in dead silence or with an audible gasp.

Now to have one of your best laughs received in either of those manners is, to say the least, disconcerting. Sheffie spoke of the possibility of having the business cut, and Carte was ap-

74

proached on the matter, but he decided to keep it in. It was Gilbert's business, we were a British company, and there was no intention on our part to be other than cleanly funny. Were we to cut it out it would be admitting, in a way, that we knew it was a little more than vulgar.

As it happened, the problem, in most of our following dates, resolved itself. The boy in question was not carried in the company, but recruited locally—as all the supers are—and after Montreal it was found, in the majority of cases, impossible to get one.

We found the same difficulty in later years in the United States, and whereas in *The Gondoliers* it didn't matter so much, and in any case relieved us of the possibility of any comments relating to vulgarity, it was a different thing as regards *H.M.S. Pinafore*, where the same procedure for obtaining the Midshipman was used. The Middy is quite an important character, Buttercup actually speaking a line to him at one point, so it was decided that we would have to carry one with us, and one of our chorus ladies—the tiniest—suddenly found herself a male impersonator.

The temperature continued down somewhere near or below zero. We had all been warned about this, and all had provided ourselves with some outer garment or other to ward off the icy blast. I had provided myself with a "trench coat" with a good thick wool lining and an oilskin lining. Before leaving England I had managed to get hold of a piece of fur—actually it was skunk—just big enough to make a fur collar that when turned up would cover my nose and ears; I also provided myself with a pair of fur-backed gloves. While waiting for a streetcar, not very long after we had arrived in Montreal, I felt a hand stroking my collar. I turned to see who it was. It was a complete stranger who said: "Say, bud, where's the dawg team?"

My Montreal stranger was not the only one to pass rude remarks to me regarding my top-winter-cum-rain-coat. Several of my own companions had already amused themselves and others at my expense, and in Winnipeg I was once greeted with: "Whatcha' doin', stranger, hibernatin'?" The end very nearly came in Regina, Saskatchewan. I left my hotel, on foot, for the theatre. I didn't think it so very cold as I left, but before I had gone very far I began to feel that pinched feeling at the end of my fingers in spite of my fur-backed gloves. My nose and ears, too, were beginning to feel the pinch. There was a thermometer I had noticed when passing the day previously, and I decided to check up on the temperature. It was 30 degrees below zero! "Hmm, no wonder it feels cold," I thought. But the theatre wasn't very far, and I soon reached it. Once inside I took off my coat, dropped it to the floor, and—it stood up. The oilskin lining had frozen stiff. When one of the stage hands learned that I had walked from the hotel he told me that it was quite probably the fur collar that had saved me from a pretty severe frostbite. I never allowed anybody to make fun of my coat again.

Our tour took us right through to the coast, our dates varying from three days to two weeks. Our week in Calgary was one of the highlights of the tour for Harry Lytton. A meeting was arranged for the whole company with a tribe of Indians. The rendezvous was some twelve or fifteen miles out of Calgary and had been arranged by the chief of the Royal Northwest Mounted Police. A troop of this very fine body of men was there waiting for us as we arrived in our cars. But disappointment awaited us. There were none of the famous red coats and broad-brimmed hats. Thick short raccoon coats and beaver hats were their uniforms. After all, it was still very cold. The Indians arrived shortly after ourselves, driving up in the Indian equivalent of the old prairie schooner or on horseback, and all decked out in their feathered headdresses and full moccasins. The chief of the tribe was an old man with a face like a piece of very old parchment. He was reputed to be well over a hundred and to have fought against the paleface during the early pioneer days. To me he seemed quite harmless, and he was more than willing to pose for his photo. I don't think he was very active as the chief, for it was a much younger man who seemed to be in control. At any rate, it was he who produced one of those full-feathered headdresses, placed it on Lytton's head, and pronounced him a chief.

We left Calgary at four in the morning—the Sunday morning following our closing on the Saturday night. I wasted no time but went straight to my berth. I wanted to be up early enough to see our entry into the Rockies. I wanted to see Banff and that amazing C.P.R. hotel that was built inside a shed artifically heated so that the men working on the building might continue with the building during the winter months. Whenever I see a picture of that hotel I always recall my first sight of it, and my first impression, which was one rather reminiscent of one's childhood impressions of the fairy castles in Grimm's and Hans Andersen's fairy tales.

Cold as it was I spent as much time as I possibly could on the observation platform drinking in the grand and awe-inspiring beauty of that mountain scenery. I don't usually grow poetic, but were I a poet then I would have all the subjects I would ever need upon which to write my verse.

I have spent time in the Himalayas, or at least on the fringe of them. I have seen Kashmir and floated down the Shalimar; I have lain in the shadows of the Yosemite Valley, and looked upon the Grand Canyon of the Colorado, but never have I seen such beauty as that afforded me by the brief glimpse I had of that jewel of nature, Lake Louise, right in the heart of the Rockies. There may be, there probably are, places in the world that can rival Lake Louise, but they will have to be mighty good to erase that picture from my mind.

As the time for our departure for England grew nearer a certain degree of reluctance to leave Canada became evident. Of course, we all looked forward to going home, but all had made several new and good friends, and had had new and exciting experiences, some a little too exciting. For instance, there was the time the whole of the staff, management, stage management, wardrobe, and orchestra had to leave Regina for Saskatoon on the night train immediately after the show on Wednesday night—they were two of our three-day dates —in order to have the show ready and the augmented orchestra rehearsed for Thursday's opening at the last-named city.

The performers left the following morning at eight o'clock. It was extremely cold, somewhere in the neighborhood of forty degrees below. It was an eight-hour journey by the day train, about twelve by night. Approximately halfway we noticed an odd coach standing in a siding way out in the middle of the prairie that appeared to us as if it had been on fire. It had, and it was the coach in which our advance party had been travelling. As soon as possible after it was discovered, the train was stopped and the whole of our party detrained. For some reason it was impossible for them to be given shelter in another coach—I think because our special baggage cars containing scenery and wardrobe lay between their sleeping car and the remainder of the train. Consequently they had to get out onto the side of the track. Some were more fortunate than others, not having had to unpack any of their bags other than an attaché case for their night things. All lost some of their clothing, overcoats, or jackets, but poor Harry Norris, who had gone to the train in his conductor's uniform, white tie and tails, was left in the position of having to turn out onto the track in pyjama trousers and tail coat. And that is pretty flimsy wear for 45 degrees below. Some kindly soul did manage to find him a blanket, and he was only there for a few minutes, five or six at the outside, but as he put it himself, "With a blazing car on one side and on the other a wide-open prairie where the bottom had damn nearly fallen out of the thermometer, it was no fun. Roasted in front and frozen behind, I had to go round like a sheep on a spit to keep an even temperature."

But that was the worst of the experiences and the only one of its kind. One experience I shall never forget was our first visit to give a concert at the Manitoba Penitentiary. About a dozen of us went. Our audience numbered between three and four hundred prisoners and a dozen guards. The sentences they were serving ranged from five years to twenty-five and life; the crimes from simple forgery to bank robbery and murder.

As an audience they were marvellous. For my particular part of the programme I sang a couple of popular songs, told a couple of funny stories, and wound up by trying to get them to sing one of the songs with me. The song in question was one very popular at the time, the chorus of which, from which its title came, began, "I scream, you scream, we all scream for ice cream, Rah, Rah, Rah." To say that I succeeded in my design is to put it mildly, for as soon as they got hold of the words and

the tune they roared it out right lustily; the big difficulty was
to get them quiet enough to permit the next turn to go on.

By the end of the concert we had practically forgotten that
we were entertaining a number of men among whom were
some dangerous criminals, but it was brought back to us rather
forcibly, and incidentally brought one of the biggest laughs of
of the afternoon, when one of the prisoners was called upon
by the chief warden to propose a vote of thanks to us; the
prisoner finished up his little speech by saying: "I am sure I
speak for all of us here when I say that we look forward to seeing you here again. . . ."

Our journey ended in Vancouver. I liked Vancouver—at
least I could have done so had we been allowed a sufficient
length of time to get to know it—but unfortunately, although
the company was there for a month, our time was divided between Vancouver itself and Victoria, Vancouver Island, to
which place we sailed every Sunday. Two years later, when
we revisited the place, we did get a chance to see more of it,
the policy of the theatre having changed, and we spent a full
month there before going over to Victoria and thence into the
United States.

On this, our first trip, we did not go down into the States but
retraced our steps with the two exceptions of Regina and
Saskatoon, finishing up in Montreal just in time to have a
perfect Canadian spring greet us. And that, after all the months
of snow and ice, was more than welcome. I should also have
mentioned rain, for Vancouver's climate is probably the nearest approach to English weather in the whole of the country.

The end of the tour came at last, and we embarked on the
White Star liner *Megantic*. Most of us had been looking forward to the sea trip, having extremely pleasant memories of

the trip out, but it wasn't until we were some days out that any of us really began to enjoy ourselves. Most of the first few days the life lines were out, and most necessary they were, as it was impossible to move around the deck, or indeed any part of the ship, without having something to cling to. For myself, once having got as far as my deck chair I stayed there until it was time to go down to my cabin to bed—an operation I was not nearly so keen on. It meant going below decks and getting undressed.

But most of us eventually got our sea legs, and those once acquired, the remainder of the voyage was thoroughly enjoyed. I am afraid that our soubrette, Aileen Davies, was one of the worst sailors and never really quite recovered until we landed. That applied on both the outward and inward voyages; and opening as we did in Montreal with *The Gondoliers*, there was a wealth of meaning in her voice when she said in the second act, "And we've crossed the sea, and, thank goodness, *that's* done!"

※ ※ ※ ※ ※ ※ ※ ※ ※ ※ ※ ※ ※ ※ ※ ※ ※ ※ ※ ※

SEVEN

Second Tour Abroad

The year of 1927–28 saw many changes. The Small Company was taken off the road and disbanded just after our return from Canada. Some of the company were absorbed into the Repertory, now the only existing company; others found work elsewhere. Ivan Menzies, for instance, eventually found his way to the Tait and Williamson Company performing G. & S. in Australia, where he has continued ever since. Leslie Rands came to us, and remained until he retired from the company in 1947. His wife, Marjorie Eyre, joined us a little later, after she had presented her husband with a son, and eventually took over the soubrette parts from Aileen Davies, who left to get married. Leo Sheffield left at the end of that year and was replaced by Sydney Granville, recently returned from Australia, who found himself playing vastly different parts than when previously in the company, when he was the juvenile lead and did the Strephons and Giuseppes.

It was also during this year that I began to go on occasionally for Henry Lytton, giving a trial show here and a trial show there. My first scheduled performance was for the Major-General in *Pirates of Penzance* while in Glasgow. The morning of the day I was to appear the death of Queen Alexandra was announced. I was fully prepared to hear that there would be no performance and that the theatre would be closed. But the theatre did not close, and there was a performance—but it was decided by the powers that be that I should not give my trial show but that Henry Lytton should appear *as a mark of respect to her late Majesty, the Queen Mother*. To tell the truth, I was not at all put out by their decision; in fact I rather welcomed it, for to have appeared that night would have been in the nature of a double ordeal. But the subtlety of their gesture has always eluded me—and, as Henry admitted to me, himself as well.

Around about this time I was playing several other parts, including Florian in *Princess Ida*, and for a while the Usher in *Trial by Jury*. And the first show I did for Henry, several years later, was after all the Major-General.

September of 1928 saw us once more on our way to Canada —with several changes of cast. Henry Lytton and Bertha Lewis were still with us, also Charles Goulding. Winifred Lawson had been replaced, and Leslie Rands and Marjorie Eyre had taken over the juvenile and soubrette roles respectively. Leo Sheffield had given way to Sydney Granville. I by this time had given up practically every other role with the exception of the Major in *Patience*—which we did not carry with us on that tour—Cox in *Cox and Box*, another we did not take with us; and the Counsel in *Trial by Jury*, a role that was given to me about three or four weeks before we sailed. I had appeared in the role some year or two before when in the Small Company. In fact, I have good reason to believe that I have created a record in that I have actually appeared in four different roles in one opera—in fact, two operas, viz.: The Associate (granted a "mute" role so far as solo lines go, but nevertheless a role that appears named on the programme), the Judge, the Usher (which I played a little later), and Counsel in *Trial by Jury*; in *The Gondoliers* I have Luiz, Antonio, Giuseppe, and the Duke of Plaza-Toro to my credit.

We sailed in the C.P.R. liner the *Duchess of Atholl*. Our trip was marked by extremely unpleasant weather beginning almost as soon as we left Liverpool and continuing until we were practically in the Gulf of St. Lawrence. The Monday night was particularly bad—or so I was told. All I knew about it was that I woke the next morning with a strained wrist. I can only explain that by suggesting that I must have been thrown pretty violently against the bulkhead to one side of my bunk (I was in an upper berth, with Sydney Granville in the lower, for which I was not ungrateful—he was a shocking sailor!), and put my hand out to save myself. Whether I was at the same time partially knocked out, that accounting for my having no knowledge of the severity of the storm, I don't know. It's possible, for the next morning I was told that even the off-watch crew, to say nothing of the passengers, had spent the night fully dressed. What happened we never found out—at least the passengers didn't—but at some time during the night, possibly the time when I was flung against the bulkhead, the ship came down with a most colossal bang, throwing practically everybody out of their bunks.

It was good to see a lot of our old friends when we arrived in Montreal. It was also very good to be greeted by a really magnificent Canadian fall. On this trip we didn't really see any winter until we arrived in Denver early in the next year. Christmas in Vancouver was so warm that I was enabled to accept and enjoy several motor launch trips up the various inlets and picnic luncheons were taken on the shore. A small party of us, including Muriel Barron, who later on made a big success with the Ivor Novello shows, used to go about together, and we made quite a few trips into Vancouver's Chinatown. Through the kind offices of a friend we were introduced to a fairly wealthy Chinese merchant, whose name I could never remember, and doubt if I could pronounce, let alone spell it. It was his pleasure to take us to dinner at one of his restaurants. It was a Chinese meal, of course, and I had not the faintest idea of what I was eating, but I, along with all the others, thoroughly enjoyed it. It was not until two or three days later that I discovered that we had been eating dog. I was very upset when I heard and told our friend that if I had known I would not have touched a mouthful. I was and am a dog lover. He explained to me that the type of dog used for human consumption was not the type one would choose as a pet. Nevertheless, that meal is registered in my mind as the one meal I could have very well done without. Nothing in the world would ever make me take such a meal again. At the same time I have a sneaking feeling that my leg might have been slightly pulled. The friend in question was not averse to an occasional practical joke, and I would not put such a leg pull beyond him. I can only hope such was the case.

After a month in Victoria we entered the United States for the first time. Prohibition had not been repealed at this time, so it was with slightly raised eyebrows that I watched a man moderately early the next morning not only drunk, but utterly incapable, being put into a taxi by a police officer. I remarked on it to one of the porters as I went out, only to learn that

"Well, ya see, liquor's illegal. Ya ain't allowed to sell it, so obviously ya can't buy it, and if ya can't buy it how in hell can ya git drunk?" And logically that's quite sound.

Personally it didn't worry me to any large extent at that time whether I had a drink or not. I must admit that as the years have progressed I do like a couple stiff ones after a heavy night's work, but there was plenty more I could do with my money then. I wasn't a teetotaler—God forbid I ever will be—but it didn't worry me that I couldn't go into a bar and order what I pleased. But never in all my life have I seen such stacks of drinks of all sorts as I saw at a party given to us by a certain club there. There was everything from champagne to moonshine, brandy to beer—and several men of no mean standing in the police force were there enjoying it.

Of all the cities I think San Francisco is one of the finest. Don't ask me why, I couldn't tell you. Like all other cities it is commercial, and what is more it is a seaport. But there is an atmosphere about it, and about the people in it. We were only there for two weeks, and to my regret I have only been back to the place once since and then only for one night in 1942 to take an R.A.F. rugger fifteen there to play one of the far too few English-style rugger teams in the United States. (I'm sorry to say that they wiped the floor with us to the tune of 28 points to 3.)

I saw quite a lot of the city while there, and was able to make trips over to Berkeley and up and down the coast with the inevitable visit to the Golden Gate. The bridge had not been built then, and when I first heard of the decision to do so I was horrified. It was going to ruin one of the finest sights in the world, I was sure—the sight of that deep golden sun going down between the tips of the two headlands and setting them

on fire. I was not the only one to think so—but we were all
wrong. I saw it in '42 both from a distance, near to, and on
the bridge itself. I am not going to say that it has improved the
view, but it has certainly not spoiled it. The designer has managed to create an impression of some rather delicate piece of
filigree which, while neither adding to nor yet detracting from
the original beauty of the scene, has a beauty entirely its own—
in particular during those last few moments when the sun
is about to sink below the horizon and puts the bridge into
the most delicate silhouette.

To go from the sublime to the ridiculous, the one thing I
could not stand in San Francisco was a homemade red wine
that could be obtained at a speakeasy practically opposite the
stage door, drunk with relish out of teacups by several of our
stage staff and orchestra. I was inveigled into trying a cupful
one day, but as far as I was concerned, one sip was one too
many. A far better use could have been made of it in one's pen,
had it been a deep shade of blue instead of red—unless one
had a penchant for writing in red ink, or worked in a bank.

With the exception of the part of Counsel in *Trial*, I was
doing nothing else than cover Henry Lytton, and playing the
matinees for him—until we reached San Francisco, where it
was decided he should play every performance, including the
matinees. Result—I was the most bored man in the city. The
boredom continued through Los Angeles. I do not include
non-matinee days in my boredom other than the evenings.
When the show was on I was thrown entirely on my own resources. Officially I was supposed to spend every minute of
the evening within the theatre in case anything happened to
Lytton. As time went on with nothing ever happening I gradually began to take a chance and leave the theatre once I had

seen him on the stage. In fact, during the whole of my period as walking, or otherwise, understudy to Henry Lytton I was only once called upon to go on for him through sickness, and that was after the accident, of which I shall speak later.

I used to spend my time going to a film show, or sitting in, or rather at, a soda fountain absorbing double malteds or some such drink, and a certain amount of American slang. In Los Angeles a lot of my days were spent in the Selig Zoo. It is here that most of the animals used in films are kept and trained. One of my pets was Leo, the Metro-Goldwyn-Mayer lion who appeared in all their titles. He was a complete darling, toothless by this time, and as harmless as your own pet pussy. Another friend was a young lion, about two years old, known as Jackie. I was eventually allowed to accompany him on his walks, where his favourite trick was to grab your leg in his jaws. One needed to be careful on those occasions not to attempt to drag one's leg away, otherwise he was likely to close his jaws. His only intention would be to retain his hold. But his teeth were big, strong, and sharp, and gently as he might have closed his jaws they would have penetrated deeply—and the taste of fresh blood might possibly have turned him from a playful and harmless animal into a dangerous brute with a taste for human flesh. At least, that is what I was told and I respected it accordingly. The procedure to adopt in those cases was to give him a sharp slap across the snout, when he would release immediately, possibly growl a bit, and continue with his walk.

Parties were given, of course, by several of the Hollywood stars. Some were constant patrons of the theatre. Charlie Chaplin was there many nights, slipping into the back of the theatre after the curtain had gone up, and out again just before the curtain came down. Reginald Denny, whose father had appeared in several of the principal G. & S. roles, gave a big party at the Paramount Studios during the time he was making the "Leather Pushers" series of pictures. It was about this time I saw, and met, one of my favourite actresses—Ruth Chatterton. The picture—*The Doctor's Secret,* one of the first full-length all-talkies, if not the first. I didn't meet Ruth again until 1951 in New York.

It is said that once you get the sand of California into your shoes you never get it out again. Well, this much at least I know—it was with some pangs of regret that I left California, and I was very glad to revisit the place again in 1941, my sojourn on that visit extending to very nearly two years. But of that, more anon.

On one occasion, in Seattle, I was vastly amused by our dresser. Those who occupied the room and shared the services of the dresser were Charles Goulding, Darrell Fancourt, Joseph Griffin, and myself. We were talking among ourselves when suddenly the dresser said: "Say, you guys talk English with a funny accent."

Goulding looked up. "Well, I don't know," he said slowly. "After all, we are English, you know, and English is our language, whereas you are an American, a citizen of the United States of America, a nation that has adopted English as its national language. Don't you think the boot might be on the other foot—that it is you who speak it with a funny accent?"

"Maybe you got sumpin' there," came the rather surprised reply. He paused, then went on, "But how come this opera company that's supposed to be English, and all the operas are supposed to be English, have to pinch one of our American college songs?"

"Which one is that?" we enquired politely.

"Why," almost seething with righteous indignation by this time, "that one in that pirate opera—'Hail, hail, the gang's all here!'" bursting into America's college version of "Come, friends, who plough the sea."

That was too much, and we dissolved into hysterical laughter. And needless to say, we did not permit the boy to foster his illusion much longer. At least, I hope we didn't. I hope that our assurance that Sullivan wrote it in 1880 was, and still is, believed.

Our journey back to the north took us through Death Valley, the sand of which I would shake most hurriedly out of my shoes, from the look of the place, for I have never seen such sheer desolation. A most aptly named district, and though it was still only the beginning of March, exceedingly warm. It came as something of a shock to wake up the next morning and find it necessary to don one's heavy winter coat and put on one's snowboots. Late that night found us in Denver, where I once again began to play the matinees in place of Henry Lytton. My first performance was the Wednesday matinee in the part of the Duke of Plaza-Toro. I think someone might have warned me that playing the Duke in Denver was a little different from playing it in Seattle or Portland. They are practically at sea level. Denver is somewhere in the neighborhood of 6,000 feet. Blithely I began to sing the opening quartet. By the end of the ensemble I was only just able to recover my breath in time to begin the second verse. When I at last set foot off the stage I was very nearly prostrate, and fully convinced I had a very serious heart condition. But one of the stage hands came and told me to take it a great deal easier until I became acclimatised, explaining that all strangers to the city were "took that way," it was just the altitude. I had the same experience in Gulmarg, about 7,000 to 8,000 feet up in the mountains of Kashmir. I was playing golf. After holing out on one green, one had to climb a matter of a dozen steps to reach the next tee. I foolishly ran up—and then had to sit down for the next ten minutes to recover.

The only real "flop" we had was in Chicago, where we went after Denver. Big Bill Thompson was the mayor at the time, and it was not so very long before our arrival that he had arranged a bonfire in which he had burned a considerable quantity of Shakespeare's works as part of a "hate" program directed against Britain. We opened, as one of the Chicago papers put it some six years later, "to the rolling of drums and a blaze of searchlights." I don't remember the rolling of the drums, but I do remember seeing the blaze of searchlights. It was a brilliant opening, if only for the light afforded by the searchlights. The house was full, and it was the last full house, or anywhere near full house, we saw for the remainder of the visit. As the same paper put it, we ". . . crept out two weeks later to less illumination than that afforded by a two-cent candle." The later visit during which this paper made those comments was originally intended to be one of two weeks and we stayed six. But then Big Bill Thompson was no longer the mayor.

My stay in Chicago on that first visit was marked for me by three incidents. Asking a "cop" how many times he had drawn his gun for the purpose of using it and receiving the answer: "Never had it out of the holster, 'cept for cleaning it." Watching a "gun duel" between a cop and some poor petty hold-up man in which I think no more than half a dozen shots were fired before the culprit threw down his gun and surrendered, and, as far as I could see, no one was in danger at any time. And, thirdly, meeting Al Capone. That was at a fashionable night club. A suave gentleman, with a great charm of manner. I suppose his bodyguards were somewhere about, but they were not evident, at least not to me.

Freddie Hobbs, who by this time had taken over the business management of the company, did once ask a cop what he should do if, while returning from the bank with the salary money, he should be held up. He was told, "Hand over all you've got. There's more in the bank, but there ain't no bank for lives." A piece of advice he fortunately never had to put into practise.

We sailed from Montreal towards the end of May, 1929, on the *Duchess of York*, the sister ship of the *Duchess of Atholl*, the one we went out in. The *Duchess of York* trip was as peaceful as the *Atholl*'s had been violent, and a good time was had by all, the usual concert taking place, and of course, the fancy dress night. For the latter I had thought up a costume that I thought not too bad. I would go as a "Dirty (K)night." I went down to the galley stores and managed to bribe one of store keepers to cut me out some armour plating from an empty coffee tin—a big twenty-pound or fifty-pound coffee tin—including a form of tin hat. This, tied on over my dinner clothes, with two or three empty whisky and gin bottles hung on, completed the costume with the exception of—a sword. Where could I get one?

After making due enquiry I was told that the first officer, a Royal Naval Reserve officer, always sailed with his sword aboard. Doubtless he would lend me his if I asked. Where could I find him? Oh, at this time he would likely be in his cabin. I thanked the purser for his information and went off to find the first officer's cabin. I knocked on his door and a voice said, "Come in." I went. The voice was on the bed and very tersely demanded to know what I wanted. I told him. When he had finished telling me what he thought about anyone who went to his cabin when he was trying to get some rest after a long spell on the bridge, and especially anyone who had the audacity to think that they could borrow a naval officer's sword just to complete some blankety-blank-blank costume, I felt I needed medical treatment to cure the blisters. He finally roared at me: "Who the hell do you think you are?" I told him, ending rather timidly with: "I'm one of the D'Oyly Carte Opera Company."

He sat upright. "One of the D'Oyly Carte. . . . Do you sing Gilbert and Sullivan?" I nodded—it was all I was capable of. "Then why the bloody hell didn't you say so at first? You can have the bloody ship!"

When I returned to the purser, sword in hand, and thanked him for his information, I had all the revenge I needed for his practical joke.

❋＊❋＊❋＊❋＊❋＊❋＊❋＊❋＊❋＊❋＊❋＊❋＊❋

E I G H T

Great Events

On June 3, 1929, Robert Courtneidge's The Sport of Kings
gave its final performance at the Savoy Theatre. As the curtain
fell on this performance and the audience began to leave the
theatre, workmen began to stream through the pass doors. Before the last of the patrons had left the theatre, the first of the
seats in which they had been sitting were being moved out
of the auditorium. The rebuilding of the Savoy Theatre had
begun.

Just over four months later a large cocktail party was given
by Mr. Rupert D'Oyly Carte to ". . . view the new and en-
larged Savoy Theatre." Three days later it was officially opened
by the D'Oyly Carte Opera Company with a performance of
The Gondoliers. The Gilbert and Sullivan operas had returned
home after an absence of twenty years.

This new Savoy was as much an innovation as the old Savoy
had been with its electric lighting for both stage and auditorium.
Indeed, so new had this electric lighting been that the builders
themselves had equipped the old theatre with complete gas
lighting as well, in case anything should go wrong. To the best
of my knowledge the whole of that gas lighting equipment was

removed with the rest of the interior in the same unused condition in which it was installed, nothing having gone wrong with the new-fangled method.

A story is told, but I do not vouch for the truth of it, and a different version is told by Mr. Leslie Baily in *The Gilbert and Sullivan Book*, that Mr. Richard D'Oyly Carte appeared in front of the first-night audience with one of the new electric bulbs in hand and explained to them that there was absolutely nothing to be afraid of; that these bulbs were harmless; if anything went wrong with the system they just went out, and even if they should break or be broken nothing more serious would happen than that that particular light would go out; and that even if they all went out, they still had the gas system. To prove this, he dropped the bulb onto the stage. The next ten minutes or so, following the resultant explosion—which, harmless though it was, was unexpected—he spent in calming a nearly panic-stricken audience. But, as we all know, electricity had come to stay, and the New Savoy has probably one of the finest switchboards in the country, if not the world.

This grand opening season of 1929 was marked by the return to the cast—for the season only—of Derek Oldham, after a lapse of several years during which he had appeared in a number of Daly's Theatre shows, including *Whirled into Happiness* with Billy Merson, Mae Bacon, Tom Walls, and Winnie Melville (whom he eventually married, and who was also engaged as principal soprano for this G. & S. season). This was Winnie Melville's only appearance with the company, but it was not to prove Derek's last. Leo Sheffield also returned to the cast to play some of his old parts.

It was a memorable season, too, for marking a terrific innovation so far as the B.B.C. was concerned. For the first time in history Rupert D'Oyly Carte permitted one of the operas to be broadcast. Strictly speaking, it cannot be said that it was the first time Gilbert and Sullivan had been broadcast, for the opera chosen was not Gilbert but *Cox and Box*. The first broadcast of G. & S. did not occur until some little time later. But it was the first time that R.D.C. had permitted any of his cast to appear on the air. The date was December 25th, so perhaps it was a case of "the better the day, the better the deed."

I was not originally engaged to play the role of Cox on the air, but I was playing it in the theatre. When I heard that Sydney Granville was to do it I took what I still think was righteous umbrage and promptly went to see Richard Collet, our general manager. He stated that he fully appreciated my views, which were that if I was good enough to play it in the theatre, then I was good enough to play it on the air. But, he said, it was not up to the company, or to Carte. The B.B.C. had said who they wanted, and one of them was Sydney Granville. (He, by the way, had played it some years before prior to his relinquishing the juvenile roles and going to Australia, so there was a proportion of right on their side.) However, I was not satisfied with Collet's explanation and demanded the name of the B.B.C. person concerned. Surprisingly, Collet gave it to me, and I went across to Savoy Hill, and demanded and secured an interview.

There I was told that it was nothing to do with them and that it rested in the hands of the D'Oyly Carte office. They said which of the performers the B.B.C. should engage. Back I went to Collet and repeated this piece of information, finishing up with: "Anyway, either I play the role in the broadcast, or you find someone else to do it in the theatre. If I'm not good enough for the one, I can't be good enough for the other. Granville had better play both."

That is one of the very few times I ever successfully held my own with the D'Oyly Carte Company. Some people called it "holding a pistol to their heads," as I knew very well Granville either could not or would not play the role in the theatre (it would hardly have gone well with his Shadbolts and other similar roles) and I also knew they had not got an understudy ready to go on. Furthermore, I knew that Richard Collet was really on my side. At least, I suspected it. I didn't know for certain till some years later, after Mr. Collet had become "Dicky," when he confessed the fact to me. Twenty-four hours later I was offered a contract by the B.B.C., and I promptly sent it back demanding more money. I got it!

Many are the sound effects I have seen in operation since then, but the whole programme was nearly ruined by the means they adopted to produce the effect of frying bacon during that show. During the rehearsals not one of the three of us had taken much notice of the effects used, and I cannot really say whether this particular effect was tried out, but at the performance proper, when the moment came to impress the listeners with the fact that Mr. Box was frying his breakfast bacon, an assistant held a glass of water close to the "mike" and solemnly tipped spoonfuls of Eno's Fruit Salts into it.

New Year's Day 1930 brought great excitement. The Honours list included the name of Henry Lytton. This was a well-deserved honour, though it was the cause of quite a lot of adverse comment. The main criticism seemed to be that Lytton was and always had been an employee and had done nothing other than continue to earn a living playing Gilbert and Sullivan. I beg to differ. Lytton had not only spent fifty years bring-

ing laughter and happiness to the British nation, but had helped
in no small way to spread Gilbert and Sullivan throughout the
world—his services to art, music, and the drama were equal
to those of any of his profession who had received similar honour. His knighthood was the cause of my appearing in his
stead for three consecutive performances in Dublin, the first
consecutive performances I had ever done for him. He had to
go to London to receive the accolade.

The next time I had to appear for Lytton was not so
joyful an occasion, and lasted for a period of close on two
months. We had been playing a four-week season in Manchester. By this time I was doing at least one show a week for
him, and had just been informed by the office that I was to
take over the part of Robin Oakapple in *Ruddigore* permanently. Lytton was somewhere around sixty-six years of age,
and it was considered that he was a little too old for the part.

Following Manchester we were booked in Cambridge for
a week. Several of the members of the company did all their
travelling by road, Henry Lytton being one and Bertha Lewis
always travelling with him. I, too, had a car and also travelled
by road. I left Manchester fairly early on the Sunday morning
and as usual took things easily. I never speeded—and please
do not say, "What never?" A modest thirty-five miles per hour
was my usual speed. There were two reasons for this: one, I
had all day to do the journey in; and two, it was a good thing
I had, as my particular vintage of car was incapable of going
any faster.

I had a leisurely lunch en route, during which I saw Lytton
go past in his Wolseley. Passing through Huntington about
four in the afternoon, I set out on the final stretch of sixteen
miles. It was raining, and the road surface was none too good.

About six miles from Cambridge I passed a car away off the road straddling the hedge bounding the fields on my left. No one was about, and beyond a glance in passing and the thought that someone had had a nasty skid I gave little or no thought to the car itself. Had anyone been there I might have stopped and learned the news then and there.

As it was, I did not hear it until somewhere about eight o'clock that night, when I was told that the car was Henry Lytton's and both he and Bertha Lewis were in hospital. Furthermore, I would probably have to go on for him the next day. I really thought I was having my leg pulled at first, but I was not. Their prophecy was only too correct. I went on and continued to do so right up to the last week of the tour, when he returned to make two or three appearances, I think more to give him back his confidence than anything else. Apart from the injuries he received, he felt the accident very keenly—for Bertha never returned.

The theatre that Monday evening in Cambridge was packed. An announcement was made that owing to a "slight accident" Henry Lytton would be unable to appear and his place would be taken by me. Gladys Gowrie would appear in the place of Bertha Lewis. Groans echoed through the theatre. It was *The Mikado*. The curtain went up. The show proceeded. Finally the curtain came down—and pandemonium broke loose. The usual one or two curtain calls to the whole company were given, and then it was brought down for the last time. The house lights were turned up; the company, including Gladys and myself, returned to our dressing rooms. But the uproar continued from the front of the house. Fred Hobbs arrived at my room. I had to put on my wig again and return to the stage. Gladys followed me on. And then for the first and only time in the history of the D'Oyly Carte Opera Company the curtain was once more raised to permit two performers to take a personal call. Gladys and I were near to tears.

On the Thursday Bertha sent for her throat spray from the theatre. She said she felt a bit of a sore throat, probably caught from lying out in the rain after she had been taken from the car, and she wanted to be all right for the opening night at Oxford the next Monday. She died the following evening, and the company suffered another great loss. Not that she and I were ever great friends; she was Henry's friend and, naturally I suppose, resented the fact that I should be gradually working my way in as he quietly gave way. But she was a great performer, with one of the most dynamic personalities and a magnificent voice.

The following tour I dropped the title of understudy in favour of the term "deputy," and was in fact playing at least three out of the seven shows a week. Three of the parts I had more or less taken over permanently, these being Robin (*Ruddigore*); Point (*Yeomen*) and the Major-General (*Pirates*). I still continued to play the Major in *Patience*, and Cox.

Then in 1932 another Savoy season was arranged. No extra cast or special engagement was entered into this time. Isidore Godfrey was in the chair in place of Malcolm Sargent as in the previous season. Charles Goulding retained the principal tenor roles; Sydney Granville played all the Pooh-Bah roles. The remainder of the cast was as follows: Rowena Ronald and Muriel Dickson, soprano leads; Marjorie Eyre, soubrette; Darrell Fancourt, bass baritone; Leslie Rands, baritone; Dorothy Gill, contralto; and of course Henry Lytton.

I had been announced as the chosen successor to Lytton after his retirement, which would take place the following year.

Frank Steward, the man to whom I was once third understudy, was engaged to cover me. This caused me a certain amount of embarrassment—unnecessarily, as it happened. But then I was not aware that Frank had actually retired from active work and was really only doing a favour. The strangest thing of all was that his contract came to an end with the termination of the Savoy season. The company went straight on to Birmingham. En route I was taken ill with the flu. I was due for three shows that week—two of *Ruddigore* and one of *Yeomen*. Henry Lytton decided that he would like to do the Jack Point, but not the Robin Oakapple. This was the first time I had been off sick, and Frank, after a whole season of just walking about, and when no longer under contract, had to be sent for for two performances. He again covered me during our 1936–37 New York season.

The opening night of the season was, I think, the most frightening ordeal I have ever had to go through. We opened with *Pirates*, and I was appearing as Major-General Stanley. Henry Lytton sat in the Royal Box. As students of the operas well know, the first thing that Major-General Stanley does, with the exception of two very short lines, is to break right into the tongue-twisting patter song, "I am the very model of a modern Major-General." My mouth was dry as a tinder-box, in fact, to quote Robert Nainby, "I was so dry I couldn't have spit a threepenny bit." I breathed a silent prayer as my cue came, and stepped on the stage, hoping to heaven that my legs would continue to support me, and that my knees would not rattle too audibly. As the second encore came to an end I breathed another silent prayer, this time of gratitude. Gratitude for the sword which is part of the costume—and which is held in front of one, point on the ground and hands resting on top of the hilt—thus affording me a third leg, so to speak. Without it I am perfectly certain I would have gone head over heels into the orchestra pit.

It was during this season of 1932 that I met my wife for the first time. It was at a party in the Savoy Restaurant. I can't say that we took a very great deal of notice of each other at that party. In fact, it was close on six months later before we exchanged more than a dozen words. I think I proposed within seven days of our second meeting, and proceeded to propose regularly each succeeding week, either by letter, phone, or word of mouth as the opportunity arose. I eventually managed to persuade her to accept an invitation to spend a long week end with the friends with whom I was staying during the Dublin visit of 1933. These very good friends, knowing how I felt towards her, wrote her people extending the invitation, I of course adding my weight.

On the Sunday she arrived, my host and hostess went off visiting for the day leaving us two alone in possession of the house and the butler. It was a delightful house standing right on the sea's edge at Dalkey, with a natural swimming pool formed by the rocks. When our kindly host and hostess returned I was greeted with a questioning raise of the eyebrows, to which I was pleased to answer: "She said Yes—but it took me all day." I often wonder whether it would have been the same answer if it hadn't been for the kindness of my friends and the romantic beauty of the setting.

We were married the following November in Newcastle-on-Tyne at 11:30 A.M. At 7:30 I went to the theatre to appear as Major-General Stanley. The Saturday matinee proved once again how appropriate Gilbert can be at times. I was "on" for Ko-Ko. Right towards the end of the second act Katisha is explaining to the Mikado that she has "just married this miserable object." The Mikado turns to Ko-Ko and remarks, "Oh, you haven't been long about it!" to which Ko-Ko replies, "No, we were married before the Registrar!"—and that was exactly what I had been only two days previously. Perhaps I put a little more emphasis into the line than usual, I don't know, but it certainly brought a big laugh.

Henry Lytton was my best man. I'm not so sure that he did not enjoy himself more than anyone else present. He kissed the bride immediately before the ceremony; immediately after the ceremony; immediately before the small reception that followed; several times during the reception; before we left; as we were leaving; and very nearly after we had left. The bride's mother came in for her share, too, not to mention the bride's best friend. Fred Hobbs tried to keep pace with him, but failed miserably.

The year 1932 was a very tragic year for Rupert D'Oyly Carte. His only son, Michael, was on the Continent studying hotel management. He had already been through the Waiters' School in Switzerland, and it has been said that even of older men there were very few who had a finer knowledge of wines. He was on his way to continue his studies in another branch of hotel business, travelling in his own open sports car with a friend as passenger. Rounding a bend, he was confronted by a motorcyclist taking the corner on the wrong side. He swerved to avoid and the car overturned. His passenger was flung clear and escaped with little worse than a broken nose, but Michael was killed instantly.

Carte was a broken man. I have never seen such grief on a man's face again. The heart dropped right out of him. His interest in both the operas and the hotel seemed to fade away.

Had it not been for Richard Collet I would not have been surprised if he had disbanded the company there and then. As it was, we saw little of him as a rule, but from that moment on he might not have existed. Michael was the apple of his eye, and now that he was gone there was nothing worth living for—at least, that was the impression I received. Michael was to have carried on both in the hotel and with the opera company. Now there was nobody. Michael's death was a great loss not only to Carte himself but, after Rupert's death, to the company.

That season was the last to take place at the Savoy for some years. A short one took place during the Second World War, but of that I cannot speak, as I was overseas with the Royal Air Force.

NINE

American Tour of 1934-35

Sir Henry Lytton finally retired from the D'Oyly Carte Opera Company in 1934. He did not retire from the stage completely for about another nine or ten months, that is, until he had done a season in pantomime at Birmingham.

His last G. & S. performance was in Dublin at the Gaiety Theatre, in the part of John Wellington Wells, the old established Family Sorcerer. Henry always reminded me of a rather mischievous boy, always up to some prank or other, and to the end he lived up to his reputation. At the finale of the opera J. W. Wells, to overcome the effects of the spell he has cast over the inhabitants of the village, must yield himself up to Ahrimanes. This he does, and the curtain comes down as Wells sinks through the stage amid fire and flame. The curtain rises again for its "first return" and Wells' boots come flying up through the trap. Down it comes again, Wells is rapidly hoisted up to the stage, and he takes his place in the centre for the second "return."

On this, his last night, Wells, in the shape of Lytton, did not reappear for the second return. Instead a large piece of white cardboard was pushed up through the trap with the words, in

very large lettering, COME DOWN AND SEE ME SOME-
TIME! The house was convulsed with laughter. The company management were bordering on apoplexy. Such a thing
had never been done before. How dare he? How . . . !
What . . . ! Never have human beings been so near literal
explosion. But there was nothing they could do about it. Nothing. It was his final performance. And Henry was as happy as
only a small boy can be when he knows he has perpetrated the
ultimate in mischief—and got away with it.

We were booked to appear in New York that coming autumn, and after a short two weeks in Brighton, where I officially
assumed the mantle of Lytton and took over all the comedy
roles, we sailed in the *Berengaria* early in September. This was
the first time the D'Oyly Carte Opera Company had been in
New York since 1900–1901. Needless to say, neither I nor any
other member of the cast had been on the previous visit. But we
had with us one former member of the company who had rejoined in the person of Derek Oldham. And here I would like to
say I never have worked with a more sympathetic partner. He
was sheer joy and pleasure to appear with on the stage, and as
a companion off stage, charming and delightful. Sydney Granville was with us, of course, also Darrell Fancourt. Muriel Dickson was our principal soprano, one of the best we ever had,
with, of course Marjorie Eyre, Leslie Rands, and Dorothy Gill.

Our opening was an ordeal. No one knew how the New
York audiences would react to us. Oh, yes, they knew their
Gilbert and Sullivan—but it was the Gilbert and Sullivan of
De Wolf Hopper and Winthrop Ames—both very fine indeed,
but not the Gilbert and Sullivan of D'Oyly Carte tradition.
After all, this was America, and they might look upon our
productions as being a little too stereotyped.

The answer to all our speculations came before the end of the first act. We had opened with *The Gondoliers*. Up to the entrance of the Duke of Plaza-Toro and his party there is no opportunity to give encores, the music carrying straight on right up to the exit of the Gondolieri and Contadine. Then the applause broke loose, and I would hazard a guess that fully sixty seconds—which is a long time—elapsed before Isidore Godfrey could begin with the ducal party's entrance music.

Then we made our entrance, were received with very polite and subdued applause, and carried on with the opening quartette "From the sunny Spanish shore." That concluded, a complete hiatus occurred. No encore had been arranged, none having ever been thought necessary. I attempted to carry on with the following dialogue, but it was obvious from the beginning that I would never be able to break through the applause. I looked at Godfrey in the pit. He looked at me—a rather blank look. I held up two fingers—hoping he would understand I was trying to suggest that we do the second verse again. Whether he understood my signal or not, he was evidently of a similar mind. Then the orchestra had to be instructed. I saw him whisper to the leader on his left, and to the leading viola, I think it was, on his right. They in turn whispered to those behind, and so it passed back to the drummer and the bassoon player respectively. Another second to gather them together, and off went the orchestra. Dorothy gave me one pained look, the Casilda resigned herself to her fate, whatever it might be, while the Luiz hurriedly began to hook on his drum again. I am glad to say that encore, the first encore for that particular number in the history of G. & S. so far as I know, and certainly during my time, went off without a hitch. But it was a bit trying at the start with nobody quite knowing what was about to be done.

The following morning's press was most eulogistic. Our immediate worries were over. We had been accepted and acclaimed. The only thing to do now was to settle down to some really hard work, and hard work it was. For the next six to eight weeks it was a case of rehearsals every morning, except Wednesday and Saturday, preparing for the next opera, and playing the current production every night, plus the two matinees.

On top of that there was the social side of our visit, which became almost as important as the shows themselves. We were all constantly in demand for official parties, banquets, club luncheons, teas, and heaven knows what. I even found myself sitting as a model to James Montgomery Flagg.

The Lotos Club of New York wanted to give a banquet in honour of the company and to commemorate the fiftieth anniversary of a dinner given to W. S. Gilbert and Arthur S. Sullivan. The menu for the dinner given to us on this occasion was drawn by Monty Flagg and consisted of the heads of Gilbert and Sullivan wreathed in cloud at the top with a full-length drawing of Sir Joseph Porter at the right hand side. Monty got me to pose for him for this—in full costume and make-up. I arrived at his studio in 57th Street at 9:30 A.M. in a taxi complete with cocked hat, gold-braided uniform, sword, and monocle, and for the next four hours stood while he drew. True, there was the odd break for a drink. The sitting over—or the standing, if you prefer it—I entered another taxi and was driven back to the theatre, where I resumed my normal appearance. To say that the taxi drivers in both instances were surprised when they saw their passenger would be an understatement. As regards Monty, whom I did not see again until the night of the banquet, I cannot do better than to quote his own words as printed in his book *Roses and Buckshot*—a title typical of the man: ". . . I was chairman of the entertainment committee. . . . On the night of the dinner I had the principals on the dais and I was toastmaster, so I looked around the table, stood up and looked again and said:

" 'There is a most important someone missing. This is very strange—where is Martyn Green?'

"A grinning, handsome young man [*his* words] opposite me said very quietly:

" 'You're looking at him, Monty.' Then I realized that I had never seen him, save with a wonderful make-up job, and had no idea of his age."

Monty Flagg was one of the eleven or twelve men who founded the Dutch Treat Club, a literary and artistic club, meeting once a week for lunch. It has no club rooms as such. The meeting takes place in a public restaurant or hotel and the room is booked for that occasion only. I have been to several of their luncheons and am the proud possessor of two of the Dutch Treat Medallions. These are about the size of a saucer, cast in plaster of Paris, and hung about the neck of the honoured guest by a length of red ribbon.

I liked New York, and on the whole I liked the people in it. Their hosopitality knew no bounds. Two letters appeared in one of the big daily papers, the first to suggest that Great Britain should let the United States have the D'Oyly Carte Opera Company in exchange for the national debt. The other, in the nature of a reply, asked the writer of the first letter if he had stopped to consider that if such an exchange were to be effected then the United States would be in Great Britain's debt.

It is true, though, that one gentleman in Boston did write and demand that the opera *The Mikado* should be banned. How could he be expected to take his wife and child to a play the theme of which was nothing more nor less than that of a weak-minded man who was willing to sell the body of his fiancée to another in order to save his own miserable life? It was immoral, to say the least. The net result was that we turned away hundreds nightly, and he got a reply in which the writer said that he fully agreed with him, in fact would go further and have several of the children's fairy tales banned, in particular that one about the girl in the red riding hood where she is represented entering a bedroom with a wolf in it.

One of the members of the company took a taxi to the Martin Beck Theatre on 48th Street, where our season was playing. It was a Monday morning, and the driver saw something that made him open his eyes wide. Never before had he seen that queue stretch out from a box office and wind its way down the street and round the corner. He asked his passenger what they were doing. She told him they were booking seats to see the Gilbert and Sullivan operas.

"They must be making a mint of dough," he said, "them Gilbert and Sullivan guys!"

Gently she explained that both Gilbert and Sullivan were dead.

"A coupla dead guys!" Pain and surprise in his voice. "It ain't fair for a coupla stiffs to make all that dough. What good is it to them? They can't spend it where they are."

It was also a taxi driver who explained to me what was wrong with New York. He came from Montana himself, he told me, and didn't like New York—but what the hell! He had been in Europe during the War. His father had a farm in Montana, but while he was away his father had died. There was nothing to go back to Montana for, so he sold out, bought a cab, and had been driving ever since—around sixteen years, that was. But New York? It stank. Why, you could drop dead on the sidewalk, and no one would take any notice. They'd just let you lay there.

Then came the final summing-up. "Do you know what's wrong with New York?" he asked. "I'll tell you. It's too goddam accumulated!"

Well, maybe he's right—but I still like it. It's thrilling, it's exciting, and it possesses one of my favourite restaurants—Sardi's on 44th Street. I am pleased to say that Vincent Sardi is, and has been for a few years, a friend of mine, and it is tradition now for my first meal in New York—it is invariably lunch—to be taken at Sardi's. I know that I am going to get a welcome second to none, and food beyond compare.

One day my wife and I were lunching there and Vincent was standing by chatting with us. The talk got onto fish. I was telling him that I had a sudden urge for some boiled hake cooked with a thick parsley sauce. My wife began to tell him how to prepare and cook it, as Vincent did not know about the fish in question, or its very English method of cooking, and he was quite interested. Our lunch over, we departed. A week later I had a note from Vincent asking if my wife and I would have lunch with him at his restaurant several days later. I was delighted to accept. We arrived, Vincent greeted us, and cocktails were served. He excused himself from sitting or taking lunch with us. After all, he still had his restaurant to attend to, keep an eye on things, you know, and he was sure we would understand. The welcome, nevertheless, was just as warm. With that he left us. A delicious white wine was brought, closely followed by—boiled hake, with thick parsley sauce, fresh garden marrow, and boiled potatoes.

He had sent to England and had the fish especially sent over on the *Queen Mary* for us.

There are other restaurants, naturally. All are extremely good. For instance, Jack and Charlie's—an amazing place, and one of which I am very fond, especially for supper after a hard show. Here again the food is excellent, and the drinks are beyond reproach, as they should be when provided by people who have spent a lifetime studying them. Charlie is now dead, I am sorry to say, and Jack has practically retired, but the brothers of both carry on and the same genial and congenial atmosphere is maintained. If one can persuade Max to take one through the building, then one is in for a most interesting three-quarters of an hour watching apparently solid walls swing back on their hinges, through which one may pass into vast cellars fully stocked with every wine possible. Max will tell you with considerable pride that they were built and used during Prohibition and never once discovered.

The Lotos Club was not the only club to give a banquet in honour of the D'Oyly Carte Opera Company. The University Club of New York also gave one, and in giving it permitted ladies, for the first time in its history, to enter those portions of the club premises reserved solely for men.

I really owe my introduction to the University Club to my wife, in spite of the fact that it is a male club primarily. My wife was, and still is, a member of the English-Speaking Union. When the secretary of the English side of it learned that we were going to New York for an extended season they promptly gave us a letter of introduction to an American member—a Mr. Edward Otheman. Ned died just before the War, to my very great regret—but not before he had introduced me to what I think I may term America's foremost amateur operatic society —the Blue Hill Troupe, of which Ned was a keen supporter and patron. They too gave parties for us. These were usually given in one of the houses belonging to one of the wealthier members.

As a rule I will avoid any party given by "fans"—especially "fans" who are also "enthusiastic amateurs"—like a plague, but when Ned invited my wife and me to the first of the Blue Hill Troupe's parties I couldn't very well refuse. I don't know how many people were present, but practically the whole of the D'Oyly Carte Company were there; I presume the whole of the Blue Hill Troupe were there together with several of their non-member friends.

As I have explained to many people, Gilbert and Sullivan was my work and not my hobby and so necessitated my thinking, talking, and singing it six days a week for forty-eight weeks of the year. When I got to a party I wanted to talk of anything but Gilbert and Sullivan. It was quickly pointed out to me that at this particular party it was their intention to entertain us. All we had to do was to sit back, relax, and listen. Someone got to the piano and began to play the overture to *Utopia, Limited*, and I promptly retired.

I eventually found myself seated alongside of Ned on the stairway outside the room wherein the entertainment was taking place. He informed me that he too, thought it was a bit thick to inflict G. & S. on us on the one day of the week when we could forget it! He then asked me if I would like a drink and promptly went to get one. The sound of music and a voice raised in song filtered through the door of the party room, and it struck me that it didn't sound a bit like Gilbert and Sullivan. At that moment Ned came running back without the promised drink.

"I think we're missing something," he said. "They're *not* doing G. and S. In fact, it's very funny."

With that I rose from my seat on the stair and together we went quietly in to the room and thoroughly enjoyed the party.

The Player's Club of New York is another that invariably invites several of the male members of the company to one of its functions. They don't give a special dinner, but we are the honoured guests at what they call a "Pipe Night"—so called because each member and guest is given a clay pipe, tobacco is placed in jars upon the table, and all are expected to smoke them. It was here I met F.P.A. (Franklin P. Adams); Marc Connelly of *Green Pastures* fame, and on my last visit but one, that is in 1947, Marion Hargrove of *See Here, Private Hargrove*. Giuseppe Valdengo, one of the principal baritones of the Metropolitan Opera, New York, was also a guest of the club one Pipe Night in 1950.

The theatrical club of New York is the Lambs. It was there that I first met "The Great Profile"—John Barrymore, ". . . this fabulous zany," as Monty Flagg calls him. I won't attempt to describe Jack Barrymore, for that would be beyond my powers, and anyway it has been done so much better by Monty himself in his own book, *Roses and Buckshot*, and by Gene Fowler in *Good Night, Sweet Prince;* but with Monty I can say ". . . you took him as he was—or else! Personally I liked him without demanding much." And I certainly agree

with Flagg when he says of the title of Gene Fowler's book—
"and I bet I know what Jack would have made of *that* title had
he ever heard it!"

When our season was in full swing, and each of the operas
had been presented once, rehearsals eased off and a little more
time became available to carry out one's social obligations. I
have frequently said that it would not be a bad thing if we had
been allowed to close the theatre and concentrate on the social side, as there seemed to be so much more of it.

We closed at the Martin Beck Theatre the week before
Christmas, reopening in Philadelphia just after Christmas Day
a week later. How I looked forward to that week's promised
rest! I finished up by booking dates for breakfast.

Following Philadelphia we went up to Boston for four
weeks, arriving there just in time to experience one of their
worst blizzards in years. It began snowing about ten o'clock
on the Wednesday morning, very lightly at first. Then it eased
off. At five it started again, and the snow was lying about two
inches deep as I crossed over to the theatre from my hotel at
7:30. When the curtain came down there was over a foot, with
deep drifts. The stage door was blocked by one and men had
to be sent round through the front of the house to dig it away
from the outside.

My wife and I were due to go out to supper, and were collected by our host and hostess in a taxi. We had to walk to the
end of the street to get into it, as it was impossible to bring it
down right to the door. Their home was no more than five
minutes in a cab, and we were there in a little over that time.
Before dismissing the cab we ordered one from the driver to
pick us up at one o'clock. One o'clock came, but no cab. Half-
past one o'clock came, and still no cab. My host phoned to

the cab company's offices. There were no cabs. Every cab in Boston was snowbound.

There was nothing for it, we would have to walk. My wife's evening frock was tucked into a pair of pink dungarees; her evening shoes were removed and a pair of rubber Wellingtons donned. Extra coats, mufflers, and ear flaps were provided. I was encased in dark blue dungarees, a 'coon coat, and snow-boots. It had stopped snowing, but the temperature had dropped considerably. It wasn't far to our hotel—about fifteen minutes' easy walking. Besides, it was really very lovely out-side. The moon was showing signs of coming out and staying out; its rays were already lighting up the snow and causing it to glisten like millions of diamonds. The snowploughs were out levelling out the surface in an effort to make it possible for traffic to move. Our way took us alongside the Common. The keen air seemed to waken us up.

"Isn't this wonderful!" cried my wife. Then she leapt from off the hard-packed snow of the snowplough-treated roadway into the soft snow at the side and completely disappeared. Owing to a dip in the ground a snowdrift of some five to six feet had formed, and she was inside it. The night air was rent with shrieks. I thought they were for help and furiously began to claw snow away with my hands, but they weren't—they were just shrieks of laughter. At that I began to laugh, and I often think it was a very good thing no one was passing that way at that time, for I am sure they would have thought I was a maniac. I know I must have looked like one, standing there in a large 'coon fur coat, muffler round my head, laughing fit to burst. The combined efforts of us both eventually brought about her release. Then we began to feel hungry—the night air, we supposed—and made our way into an all-night restaurant, where we sat down to a large plate of bacon and eggs, toast, and coffee. We reached our hotel at 4:30. Yes, it was only about fifteen minutes' easy walking.

The following Sunday we were invited to go riding by the daughter of a friend, Professor Barbour, and John D. Roosevelt, the youngest son of Franklin D. Roosevelt, who was then serving his first term as President. John was up at Harvard. Promptly at nine A.M. Barbara picked us up at the hotel. I noticed that she was dressed in pretty heavy clothing, with rubber boots on. I asked her if it was very cold—it looked that way.

"Oh, no," she told us, airily. "Nothing to speak of."

We were wearing ordinary English hacking kit with leather top boots. Our horses were wearing studs—quite normal on snow or frosty ground. We mounted, and off we went. There was at least half a mile of road to traverse before we reached anything like a bridle track—and that's as far as I went. Never have I been so cold in my life. I had no hands and no feet, and I was not too sure whether I had a body. It was even too cold for the horse. She started on her toes, relaxed onto her flat hoof, and finished up sliding around on four balls of ice that had collected inside the shoe. Whatever she did, I had to let her, as I had no control. Barbara wasn't too bad; John wasn't too happy, and my wife was in much the same state as I. We turned the horses and made our painful way back to the stables. I had to be lifted off, and I'll swear that for fully fifteen minutes after I was removed I retained my riding position. I'd been frozen into it. It took three very large and very hot rums to get the thawing process started. I did not ride again until the snow was off the ground, and that was not until we had left Boston.

One of my favourite haunts in Boston is the Tavern Club, to which I was introduced by Owen Wister, the author of *The*

Virginian. The Tavern Club lies in a little backwater of a street off Boylston, and is most appropriately named. They invariably give a dinner to a limited number of the male members of the D'Oyly Carte, and I think I may say that it has always been one of the highlights of our visit. It is always a dinner-jacket affair, mainly, I suspect, so that the members may wear their club waistcoats. These are of various colours and indicate the decade in which the member wearing it became a Taverner.

The members of the club are mostly professional men. All would appear to be not only patrons of the theatre, but also no mean performers themselves. This is proved by the fact that following the dinner given to us the whole of the company present repair to their theatre on the top floor, where *they* set to work to entertain *us*—and right royally and well do they do it. It is arbitrarily stated that on no account will we, the members of the D'Oyly Carte, be allowed to lift a finger other than to lift a glass to our lips, or up a voice except to call for our glass to be refilled. But have you ever known any tenor or baritone —or comedian, come to that—who could sit through a whole evening's entertainment of that description and not insist on singing or telling a funny story?

Rainy days I would go into the Club about twelve noon, sometimes a little before, and endeavour to learn the game of "cushion," or "continental," billiards. My tutor was generally Gluyas Williams, whose cartoons are well known in England as well as in the States. By one o'clock I had probably "been to the table" about twice, making a score of never more than ten and generally less than five. Gluyas, in the meantime, had walked miles round the table making strokes here and strokes there, piling up a formidable score, the whole time giving me a running commentary on how the game was played, how to coax the balls into the right position, and so on, and so on. In other words giving me a practical illustration of—as he himself put it—the result of an ill-spent youth.

"But Martyn," he would say, "it's as easy as drawing."

But, you see, he was the Club champion—and besides, as I pointed out, I can't draw either. He wasted no time in telling me that he couldn't sing.

During this stay in Boston I was elected an Honorary Professor of English at Harvard. I doubt whether the professorship is recorded in any college catalogue, but here is how it happened. Frank Hersey had invited me to speak to his English class at Harvard one afternoon on the subject of G. & S. I didn't know Frank at the time, the invitation being passed on to me via Leonard Rooke, the company's press relations manager. Coming from him, it was not so much a request as a suggestion that this was something I "ought to do, old boy. This is Harvard, y'know."

There were few things I wouldn't do for Leonard, who was, without a doubt, one of the most generous men it has ever been my good fortune to meet. I'd known him for close on twelve years by this time. Any "suggestion" of his was an order from the quarterdeck so far as I was concerned, so I accepted. It was arranged that Frank Hersey should pick up my wife and me at our hotel. I spent nearly a week thinking up and typing out a lecture on the chosen subject, and was just putting the final touches to it when Professor Hersey was announced over my phone as waiting down below.

I hurriedly finished off, grabbed my hat and coat, helped my wife on with hers, and shot down to the lobby. I was about two minutes late, so without wasting any time we bundled into his car and off we went Harvardwards. About halfway there I suddenly realised that I had left a very necessary portion of my "make-up" in a glass of water on the shelf in my bathroom. I could not carry on without it, and so we had to return. That made us something like ten to fifteen minutes late in arriving at the lecture room. The students were all assembled—had been for at least five minutes before the scheduled time of starting. Frank Hersey made no bones about it. He began to introduce me immediately, commencing with an apology for being late and *explaining why!* That brought a subdued titter, quickly silenced—I presume for fear of appearing rude before a visiting lecturer. They are nicely behaved boys, those Harvard boys—and I eventually rose to my feet.

Professor Hersey's introductory preamble brought to my mind a story which I don't propose to repeat here, but which brought a resounding laugh, for which I was very grateful. Then I suddenly realised that I had forgotten something else in the rush to reach the lecture room: I had left all my notes and carefully thought-out talk in the professor's car. I had forty minutes to fill in. The only thing I could do was to carry on telling stories. I told them every one I could possibly think of. Old, very old chestnuts, hoary chestnuts; stories which my father, I know, must have dribbled down his bib laughing at. Somehow I managed to fill in the requisite forty minutes. When I sat down I fully expected to receive a pretty good ticking off from the professor. But no. He called upon one of the students to propose a vote to thanks. His vote of thanks consisted in suggesting to the professor and the rest of the class that the only way in which thanks could really be expressed, so far as he was concerned, was to put it to the class that "Mr. Martyn Green be here and now elected an Honorary Professor of English of Harvard University." Hersey beamed, rose to his feet, and put the motion to the class. It carried unanimously.

Not only was I made an honorary professor at Harvard, but once, in my alter ego as Lord Chancellor, I was invited to sit on the bench at one of the Michigan state courts. Furthermore, it was specially requested that the Lord Chancellor should wear his robes and wig. Permission was sought from the powers that be—and that rule the Lord Chancellor's comings and goings so far as the D'Oyly Carte Opera Company is concerned—by the judge who had issued the invitation, but he was met with a prompt and very direct refusal. It had been the judge's intention to introduce the Lord Chancellor to the Court before the more mundane proceedings of the day started, and if possible to get him to deliver one of his famous judgments "given *andante* in six-eight time" as an example to the court of how judgments should always be delivered. But it was not to be! Ah me! I would have liked to sit on the bench in America.

It was during this 1934–35 visit to the United States that we revisited Chicago. Because of the debacle of 1929, I was a little nervous, and it was with some trepidation that I made my entrance as Ko-Ko on the opening Monday night.

For years the traditional way of singing "Titwillow" had been inclined towards low comedy, with comical gestures and business between Katisha and Ko-Ko. The reason for that is probably that George Grossmith had no voice and was unable to do it in any other way, as for the same reason, probably, he treated the final scene of *The Yeomen of the Guard* as a piece of comedy. After I took over the parts I gradually eliminated most of the comic business, but retained the use of the falsetto voice on the last "O willow, titwillow." While in Washington, D.C., just a little prior to reaching Chicago, I had received a letter of the "fan" variety that at the same time criticised me for ruining a very beautiful song by trying to be funny. The song, of course, was "Titwillow."

By the time the curtain fell on the first act of this opening night things seemed to be going along all right. I recalled this letter and promptly sent for Isidore Godfrey, our musical director, and told him I intended to sing this song absolutely straight and would he, could he, please arrange for the strings to be muted so that I could take it very quietly. He demurred at first, but at last gave in on condition that I accepted all responsibility and took any rockets that would undoubtedly, he thought, come from the office. I accepted those conditions. There were two encores, and one of the following morning's papers came out with a double-header right across the centre pages: "MARTYN GREEN SINGS NEW SONG HIT—TITWILLOW."

I have never ceased to be grateful to my correspondent, and have sung it that way ever since. If there were any rockets from the office I never heard them. Thus may tradition be swept aside—though to me such as that is not tradition. Tradition, to my way of thinking, means the intelligent representation of the author's—or composer's—intentions, and I do not think the introduction of comedy business in that song carried it out. In fact, sung "straight" I believe more true comedy is apparent in the number. It should bring the audience to the point of not knowing whether to laugh or cry.

One of my free afternoons I went across to another theatre to see and meet Charlotte Greenwood. She laughed at the fears we'd had and prophesied—we were then just towards the end of our first week of a scheduled two weeks' booking—that we would be in Chicago much longer than we expected. We were —by four weeks.

TEN

Ko-Ko Business

Two years later we opened again at the Martin Beck Theatre.
The Mikado was the opera chosen to open with. On this occasion there were no fears as to our reception. We were sold
out for the whole of the announced programme, which was
for a period of four weeks, with people clamouring to know
if we intended staying longer and what was the programme if
we did. We had taken the whole of the repertory with us this
time. On the previous visit *Patience* had been left behind, as it
was not considered popular enough to warrant inclusion. Before the end of the first four weeks it had to be sent for and
turned out to be one of the most popular. This lesson having
been learnt, nothing was left behind on this second trip. It was
our longest absence from England to date, for we sailed early
in August, opening on the 20th, and did not arrive back in England until the beginning of June the following year.

Once again, Derek Oldham was with us as principal tenor,
and John Dean in the secondary tenor roles. Dorothy Gill had
been replaced by Evelyn Gardiner, and Sylvia Cecil returned
to the company to replace Muriel Dickson, who left us to continue her career in New York, making a very successful ap-

pearance as the soprano lead in *The Bartered Bride* at the Met.

I don't think I shall ever forget that opening night, for several reasons. In the first place, New York in August is not the coolest of places, and the Martin Beck Theatre did not have air-conditioning at this time. Instead, two very tall fans at the back of the auditorium were kept running the whole time, but all they seemed to achieve was merely to disturb the air without cooling it, yet setting up quite a draught and letting forth a rather aggravating whine during the whole of the performance.

The D'Oyly Carte are quite rightly famous for the beauty and extreme freshness of all their costumes. The costumes are famous, within the company, for their sturdiness and ability to stand up to constant packing and unpacking. To achieve this, it is obvious that good, heavy, hard-wearing materials must be used, and of the best quality. A very laudable thing—but the donning of such clothing, which in many cases arctic explorers might envy, in a theatre in New York in August, coupled with a fairly heavy part to act, sing, and dance, is not conducive to coolness. By the end of the evening I was a limp rag.

I was not far off being in that condition before the curtain. I don't think I have ever felt so many butterflies fluttering about in my stomach as I did that night. Nor have I been as near shedding tears of gratitude. The reception I got when I made my entrance was tumultuous and lasted what to me seemed an eternity. In actual fact, I do not suppose it was more than thirty seconds, but it was the first time such a welcome had ever been accorded me, and I was truly grateful.

When I got back to my room after the fall of the curtain I found a very good American friend waiting to see me. He was full of regrets at not having been able to be present for our opening, but he had only got back into New York during the evening; in fact, he had come right along from the station. I gave him a drink and started to take off my make-up when a knock came at the door. Albert, my dresser, went to see who it was and what was wanted. After a few words he gently closed the door and told me there was a guy—er—a gentleman, an Englishman, who wanted to see me. "He says you don't know him, but if you could spare a moment he would just like a word."

I asked Albert how he knew it was an Englishman.

"He's got on a top-hat, one o' them shiny things," he answered, "and he's wearing an eyeglass."

I said to show him in, and right enough, he was wearing a monocle and was an Englishman. He was an elderly person, and extremely garrulous. To misquote Gilbert, " 'e meant well, but 'e didn't know." My American friend was not holding me up at all. I could continue with my dressing for the street while he was there. Not so with my very garrulous English visitor. I stood and listened for some time, smiling politely and saying "Yes" at, I hoped, appropriate moments. At length he said:

"You know, sir, I think I must have seen *The Mikado* forty times or more, and I enjoy it more every time I see it."

Before I had time to say anything my American friend came in with:

"You know, in the United States, if we don't get it the first time we give it up."

I was a little surprised, and after my visitor had gone (incidentally, he took the remark in really very good-humoured fashion), said so in no uncertain manner. At the same time I had to agree that if drastic action had not been taken I might very well have still been there the next morning.

After the performance that same evening Martin Beck gave a smallish party for the company in the Lincoln Hotel. I was introduced to a tall, dark, and handsome woman—a Marion Ross, by name, who many years later—in 1950 to be exact—was to become not unknown for her singing of "June Is Bustin' Out All Over!" Marion gave several parties for us that visit. It was in her apartment that I first heard the music of George Gershwin's *Porgy and Bess*. Derek and I stood by the piano while Milton Rettenberg played us the score right through, with several repeats. Two of the numbers I liked particularly— "A Woman Is a Sometime Thing" and "It Ain't Necessarily So."

Two or three nights later, Marion and Milton were in the front row of the orchestra for *H.M.S. Pinafore*. I, as Sir Joseph, take on with me a roll of three sheets of music. It is "a song that I (Sir Joseph) have composed for the use of the Royal Navy." I hand it to Ralph Rackstraw (Derek Oldham) with the suggestion that he hum it at his leisure.

This particular evening I had a bit of the devil in me, and knowing that these two were in front I pencilled on the top of each sheet, in letters heavy enough to be read by them, the two titles I particularly liked and one more, "I Got Plenty of Nothin'." I also rolled them in such a way that none of the three singing it would see the words until they turned the sheets over for the second verse. Marion and Milton collapsed in their seats. Derek wondered what the laughter was about, and so did the others. The verse ended, the sheets were turned—and Derek collapsed. He had "A Woman Is a Sometime Thing." The other two, not knowing about the party, were not so amused, which was probably a good thing, as Derek did not sing a note of the second verse.

It was another party at Marion's apartment that was responsible for my "little fan business" in *The Mikado*. It came about in this way.

Sir Hubert Wilkins, the noted explorer of the Arctic and Antarctic regions, was in New York for a while and visited the theatre, after which a party was given him by a friend of Marion's who loaned her apartment for the occasion, to which Sylvia Cecil, Derek, Isidore Godfrey, my wife, and I, were invited. Each guest was presented with a small present as he went in. Mine, on opening, turned out to be a very small celluloid fan, suggestive of Ko-Ko in *The Mikado*; Derek's, if I remember rightly was a Yeoman's (of the Guard) hat; Sylvia had a small parasol indicative of Mabel in the *Pirates*, and Sir Hubert Wilkins, a block of ice made of plastic.

The day after the party Marion Ross and Milton were once again seated in the front row at the Martin Beck. The show was *The Mikado*. I was rather wondering whether I could think anything up to give them a personal laugh when my eye fell on the small celluloid fan. I at once had an idea. During one of the encores to "Here's a how-de-do" I palmed the thing in my right hand—I had always been fond of indulging in easy feats of legerdemain—and right at the end of the number, when I was standing directly in front of them, I quietly "disappeared" the normal fan and produced the little one in its place.

Not for a moment did I think it would strike anyone as funny other than Marion and Milton. They knew the history of it, the rest of the audience did not. Furthermore, I did not really think anyone beyond the front row would be able to see it, not to recognize it for what it was. To my surprise, the whole house rocked. As for my two friends, they practically performed another disappearing feat under their seats. And Derek Oldham—well, once again I must plead guilty to being the cause of a complete "dry-up" on his part.

From that it was obvious that this small fan could be seen from every part of the house, and I continued to use it, never failing to bring a big laugh. One day I mislaid it, so I hurriedly cut down one of the normal fans to half size. It served its purpose but was not quite as good as the very little one. Then I found it again. As I was preparing to go on I caught myself wondering if the two of them could not be used to advantage— the half-sized one first, and at the next encore exactly the same trick but with the still smaller one. I thought I'd try it. I did. Result—we had to take another encore!

Speaking of *The Mikado* brings to my mind the day I had an extra spice of the devil in me that generated an intense urge to "dry up" Evelyn Gardiner, the Katisha. She and I had worked hard to make the scene we had together go well, and I think we succeeded. There was one piece of business where originally, so far as I know, Ko-Ko flung his arms around Katisha's neck just as he finished declaiming the line ". . . for years I have loved you, with a white-hot passion that is slowly but surely consuming my very vitals!" whereupon Katisha flung him off. Ko-Ko would stagger back a pace or two and then collapse on his sit-upon, from where he would deliver his next line: "Ah, shrink not from me!"

This was always good for a laugh. But as Gilbert himself said, "Anyone can raise a laugh by falling on their backsides" —and somewhere around 1934 J. M. Gordon cut this business out and substituted that of Katisha turning on Ko-Ko like a tigress while Ko-Ko backed hurriedly away, delivering his

"Ah, shrink not . . ." line as soon as she came to a stop.

With this urge to "dry up" Eve I began to think out some means of doing it, and eventually hit on this spot. Without saying a word to anyone, except one of the stagehands, whom I co-opted to make sure that nothing would collapse in the way of scenery, I went on and played the scene normally up to that point. Then, as she turned on me, I waited not upon the order of my going but turned tail and fled, made one leap at one of the "flats" (those pieces of scenery that mask the sides of the stage while providing exits and entrances) and climbed up as far as I was able.

It brought, as it has brought ever since, one of the biggest laughs in the whole series of operas. As for Evelyn, I succeeded beyond my wildest dreams. She stood for a moment transfixed, and then began to laugh. She shook with her laughter, until tears were streaming down her face—and the more she laughed, the more the audience did. I must have been clinging to that piece of scenery for fully sixty seconds, maybe more, before I could deliver my next line, "Ah, shrink not from me!" which brought another gale of laughter. At last we were able to carry on with the scene, and it was fortunate that I had several more lines to say before Eve herself had to speak, thus giving her a moment or two to control herself; though even then she found some difficulty in speaking her lines smoothly.

After the curtain had come down on the show, and before I had time to leave the stage, the Business Manager, Freddie Hobbs; the Stage Manager, Harry Arnold; and the Musical Director, Isidore Godfrey, were all demanding to know what I meant by doing a thing like that. Had we been in England, J. M. Gordon would have been round as well. Never have I seen such shocked faces in my life; I might have just committed a most horrible murder—and in their minds, I believe I had. I had murdered "tradition."

"I just felt like it." I told them. "And after all, it did bring a colossal laugh. Besides, it is not out of place—Ko-Ko is in rather the same position as a treed cat."

Well, they would have to report it. Richard Collett had either arrived or was just due to arrive, and the whole incident was reported to him. We were not doing *The Mikado* again for a week or more, and I gather Dicky sent a long cable or air mail letter to Carte on the matter. To my intense surprise he came to me some days later saying that Mr. Carte had said I was to keep in whatever business I was doing at that point, and he would see it for himself on our return to England and Sadlers Wells. There wasn't very long to wait, as we were in Boston at the time, and sailed from there only a few weeks later.

I am told that Carte nearly split his sides laughing when he at last saw the "business" and within another week or two a special brace with a couple of helpful rungs was fitted to the flat in question to ensure that no damage to either scenery or myself would result.

And that is how I introduced "climbing the scenery"—a piece of business that I am told many of our patrons in the past have endeavoured to emulate when they reached home after the show—using the dining-room door. I can only trust that irate wives, or parents, do not put the entire blame on me.

And this, in turn, brings to mind the "motorcar" business, which was not originally intended to be a motorcar at all. Those who have seen *The Mikado* will remember that on the first encore to "Here's a how-de-do" I exit at one side of the stage, and, by virtue of running madly round behind the backcloth, dance on singing my verse of the number from the other side. The second encore I am to be seen crossing from one side to the other just in front of the backcloth, hopping on one foot, the big baggy trousers of my costume more or less giving the appearance of my sliding along. As the encores grew in number I wanted to find some other manner of making an entrance, and I wondered whether the baggy trousers and large sleeves would mask me in sufficiently to give the appearance of a very short man if I got down on my haunches. I tried it one night, but the critics next morning alluded to my entrance "on a scooter." A few modifications, and the "motorcar" was born.

E L E V E N

Filming The Mikado

*The world is poorer to-day by the loss of one of the outstand-*ing Gilbert and Sullivan performers of his time, and possibly of all time. I speak of Leo Sheffield, whose sudden death, at the age of 77, was announced on 3rd September, 1951. I never saw Fred Billington, unfortunately, but many who did compared Leo with him in a more than favourable light. I saw, and knew, all who followed him, however: Sydney Granville, Hilton Ley-land (who played the roles in the Small Company), Richard Walker, Richard Watson, and the latest comer—Fisher Morgan. All were good, and all, I think, will agree with me that "Sheffy" was tops.

I had a great affection for "Sheff," and I believe he had some little regard for me. Not because I was I, but mostly on account of my father. In their early days they were good friends, meeting when they were both members of the same church choir in London, and remaining good friends in spite of their chosen ways being widely divergent—my father to oratorio and Sheff to the stage.

He was an irritable old so-and-so, but so, too, were Billy (Fred Billington), Granny (Sydney Granville) and Dick

Watson. It has been said that there was something in the Pooh-
Bah parts that seemed to affect all who played them. True it is
that all—well, nearly all—eventually became tarred with the
same brush. I cannot say that it affected Richard Walker to the
same extent, but then that may be because he did not spend
quite so many years in them as the others, and Fisher Morgan
is only just commencing. But they were all likable, and in
Sheffy's case, lovable personalities.

Fred Billington was inclined to be overbearing, especially
towards the end of his association with the company. He would
brook no interference; he could and would be extremely rude
on the slightest, and sometimes without any, provocation.
Dewey Gibson, of the golden tenor voice, once told me of how,
at the old Royal Court Theatre, Liverpool, he came off the stage
and took what was known as "the short cut" back to his dressing room. He had a change and wished to save time. The "short
cut" took him through Billy's room, where he was seated at his
place (Lytton dressed in the same room but was on the stage
at the time). Just as Dewey, who had knocked before entering
and received a "Come in" which he acknowledged with a
"Thank you," was about to go out through the far door, Billy
bellowed at him:

"Where do you think you're going?"

"To my room, Billy," said Dewey.

"Oh, are you?" thundered Billy. "Well, get back the way
you came. This is my dressing room, not a bloody right of
way."

"I'm going to my room—this way." said Dewey, quite firmly.
"Apart from the fact that I have a change, and this is the quicker
way, if you think that you can intimidate me the way you intimidate all the others, you're making a big mistake."

With that he turned to go out of the room. Billy stopped him with a thunderous roar.

"Come here!" Even Dewey was a little overawed. He "came there."

"Damn it, put it there. I like you. You're the only person who has had the guts to answer me back in years. Use the damn room as a passage any time you like—and you needn't bother to knock, either. And come and have a drink when the curtain falls."

Can one help liking a man like that?

It is said of Billy that he frequently remarked that he couldn't think of a better way of shuffling off this mortal coil than by having a good glass of sherry, a rattling fine lunch with a decent bottle of wine, some black coffee, a glass of liqueur brandy and a fat cigar, and then passing quietly away.

In 1916 the company was at Cambridge. Mr. Carte sent for Billy to come up to London and have lunch as he wished to have "a chat." Billy arrived at the Savoy on time and they lunched—a glass of sherry, a good lunch with a bottle of decent wine, some black coffee, a liqueur brandy and a fat cigar. Billy was feeling fine. Over the coffee and liqueur Carte told Billy that he thought the time had come for him to retire (Billy was about seventy-odd) and that he, Carte, was making arrangements for him to do so at the end of that tour, approximately some eight to ten weeks from then. Billy listened; there was not much else he could do, and little, if anything, he could say. The "chat" over, a cab was ordered and Billy was driven to the Great Eastern Station to catch a train for Cambridge. He alighted, paid the driver, and collapsed in a porter's arms. They took him into the Great Eastern Hotel, but Billy never recovered. He died a short while after they took him in. One can only assume that the shock of the chat had been too much. He had not expected it and was not prepared for it—but—he died as he would have wished.

Sheffy was much like Billy. Perhaps his roaring was not quite so roarful nor so loud. But he could lose his temper, and very frequently with himself. Especially on the golf course. I was playing with him one day at Morton Hall, Edinburgh, the course that runs alongside the famous municipal links, Braid Hills. We had reached the fourth tee, I think it was. The tee was then situated on a fairly high bank, and the line to the green more or less a "dog-leg" round the side of a lake. Long-hitting players, and optimistic ones, would take the short line and go across the corner of the lake, which, if they carried it, put them on the edge of the green in one. Sheffy decided to take the short line, and he promptly went into the lake. "Huh," he grunted, and unwrapped a new ball. Again he attempted the short line, and again he went into the lake. Four or five times more he did the same thing and with a new ball. I think he would have gone on, though both his caddie and I had tried to dissuade him after his second attempt, had he had another ball in his bag. As it was, with a face as black as thunder, he stalked off the tee and made his way to a spot approximately opposite the place where all his balls had gone in. Then he turned, seized his bag of clubs from the caddie, turned again, and faced the lake.

"You've got every ball I possessed," he shouted at it. "Here, take the bloody clubs as well." And in they went. We spent the next half hour recovering them. Once he had them back in his hands he stalked off back to the clubhouse without so much as a good-by or a go to hell. There was little I could do but follow him, which I did with a certain amount of ill feeling for having spoiled my game. Arriving at the clubhouse, he did not go in, as naturally I expected him to do, but made his way round to the professional's shop, where he bought himself a further half-dozen balls. On coming out he called out to me:

"Sorry about all that—let's go and finish the game."

Well, there was nothing to be gained by refusing, and I wasn't tied to time, so I acquiesced. Reaching the fourth tee once more, he took out a ball, unwrapped it, and set it on the tee. With a face like grim death he took out his driver, and with a muttered "I won't be beaten by the ruddy hole," proceeded to address the ball with every appearance of knocking it into the middle of the next parish. It was obviously useless for either the caddie or me to make any attempt to stop him, so we prepared ourselves for the worst. Suddenly he stopped waggling and growled at us:

"Well, why don't one of you tell me I'm a bloody fool?" And with that he replaced his driver in the bag and took out an iron, altered his direction a little and proceeded to send the ball some hundred and eighty yards or more down the middle of the fairway to the right of the lake.

"There you are," he said, after watching the flight of the ball to its end. "Why didn't I do that in the first place? If I had I wouldn't have lost a single ball, and I'd have kept my temper."

It turned out to be one of the most enjoyable games I ever played. On our eventual return to the clubhouse—incidentally, I won the game and the half-crown that went with it—he paid the caddie for *two* rounds with the injunction:

"Never lose your temper on a golf course—you only make an ass of yourself."

As with Billy, how can one help liking a man like that?

Sheffy was still in harness when he died. Leaving the company in 1927 to make a film, which unfortunately never saw the light of day—it was a "silent" and was completed just in time to be too late, for the "talkies" had arrived—he continued to appear in musical plays until 1946. From then on he devoted his time to producing amateur societies in the Gilbert and Sullivan operas, travelling as far afield as Ireland to do so. Once asked to what he attributed his perennial youthfulness, he said:

"When a man becomes elderly he either flies to Dr. Voronoff [famous at the time as the "monkey gland" surgeon] or subsides into life's fireside chair and old age. But my elixir is a simple remedy, to be taken neat. At middle age—find a new interest."

I think he was right. I'm trying it myself.

The beginning of the summer of 1938 brought us to the Scala Theatre for a season, the highlight being the reproduction of *The Sorcerer*. It also brought us to the film of *The Mikado*. Discussions had been going on for some time between the interested film-makers and D'Oyly Carte. A company was formed under the name of G. and S. Films, Ltd., with Geoffrey Toye as the producer and director of music. He had already been associated with the D'Oyly Carte Opera Company in the capacity of musical director during the 1919 and 1921 seasons at the Prince's Theatre.

Originally the intention had been to film *The Yeomen of the Guard*, and a shooting script had been prepared. At least, when I was first spoken to regarding the making of a film it was a script of *Yeomen* that he discussed with me. Why the decision to change to *The Mikado* was taken I do not know, but it was. Let me confess, my first reaction to that decision was one of disappointment, and I am still of the opinion that it would have made a better picture than *The Mikado*. It is not my intention to make any criticisms of *The Mikado*, it is merely that I think the story of *The Yeomen* would have adapted itself better to the medium of the film than the other did. In my poor opinion the script, as I saw it, proved my contention. Of course it may be that I had a sneaking preference for Jack Point over Ko-Ko, but bear in mind, I only say—may be.

We had a lot of fun making the picture, but it involved a lot of hard work. Victor Schertzinger was engaged to direct, and Kenny Baker was engaged to play the role of Nanki-Poo. John Barclay was in the title role of *The Mikado*, with Jean Colin as Yum-Yum and Constance Willis as Katisha. The only active principals of the D'Oyly Carte Opera Company to be engaged were Sydney Granville, who proved himself a very fine film as well as stage performer; Elizabeth Paynter and Kathleen Naylor as Pitti-Sing and Peep-Bo respectively; and myself. Gregory Stroud—the Pish-Tush—had been with the company for a short while playing the juvenile baritone roles during the '26 season at the Prince's Theatre and had only recently concluded a long contract in Australia with the Tait and Williamson G. & S. Company there. In addition to these, the whole chorus was engaged in toto.

All the music was recorded first and later shot to a playback. Not a too difficult thing to do, nor yet very simple, particularly as regards one of my own songs—"Titwillow." It was desired that Ko-Ko should, at the line "He slapped at his chest . . ." emphasize the line by suiting the action to the word. It so happened that on the chosen recording the noise of the slapping action—done with the open hand on my chest—came in between the two words "slapped" and "at." Before the scene was shot I sat in front of a loud speaker while they played the record at me with myself singing it at the same time. Facing me were

Victor Schertzinger, Gene Milford, and Phillip Charlot, the two chief cutters, all watching my mouth to see that I was with it the whole time, and my hand slapping my chest to make sure it synchronized with the sound on the recording.

I wouldn't care to say how many times I went through it before they were satisfied, nor how many "takes" were necessary before all were agreed that perfect synchronization had been obtained in conjunction with a "good take" in all other respects. We were all day on the job, and when I eventually retired to my room to take my wig and make-up off I felt more like something the dog had had on the mat than a human being.

Recordings began at the beginning of our last four weeks at the Scala. They were all done at Pinewood Studios, beginning each morning at 10 and ending at any time between 5:30 and 6 in the evening. That meant I was on my way there in my car by 8:30; on my way back to the theatre by 6, and beginning another two and a half to three hours' work by 8 to 8:15. There was little time for leisure.

But that was not the worst of it. Recording over, shooting started. I decided, on the advice of Victor, that it would be a good thing if I moved out to Pinewood and lived in the club attached to the studios right away, instead of waiting until our Scala season ended, as had been my original intention. I was aided in this decision by the fact that I was due in the make-up room any time between 4:30 and 5:30 A.M., and I couldn't see myself getting up around 2 o'clock in the morning in order to get there. So, on my day off, I packed and my wife and I moved out.

For the next two weeks my schedule was more or less as follows: Rise, 4 A.M.; make-up room, 5 A.M.; make-up completed, 7 A.M.; breakfast, and if possible, snatch a few more minutes of sleep, and on the set by 9 until 6 P.M. with a break for lunch of anything from one to two hours. Remove make-up, snatch a light meal, drive into town, make up and play a show, remove make-up, dress, and start driving back about 11 to 11:15. Pinewood by midnight, a hasty and light meal and a drink, and—so to bed for a good four hours' sleep. I kept that up, with the exception of matinee days, for two weeks.

The Monday after we closed at the Scala I made my way into the make-up room at my usual time. Ernie Westmore was there waiting. I sat down in the chair and he adjusted my skullpiece and generally carried on with the job of making me up.

The groundwork completed, he began on my eyes.

"Look at the ceiling," he said.

I did—and fell right out of the chair in a state of complete collapse. When I recovered I was in my bed, and there I remained, to the consternation of the whole of the executive staff, for the next three days. I was upsetting the whole of the shooting schedule. It incidentally taught me a lesson at the same time. It taught me that so long as I was willing to go in at 4:30 or 5 every morning, they would let me. I decided against. To this end I bearded first Victor Schertzinger and then Geoffrey Toye in their respective lairs and told them that in my opinion a form of roster would not be a bad thing, thus ringing the changes on the "early turn," and as I had been on it for the past two weeks they could put my name on the late turn for the next two.

I didn't waste time arguing. I just went to my doctor, who told them in no uncertain terms that "unless, . . . , etc., etc.," I would probably collapse completely. I'd had no rest for the past twelve months, and would not be getting any for the next twelve. A roster was drawn up and agreed to, and from then on—a good time was had by all.

Victor, whom I got to know very well, was about the most patient man on the set I've ever met. Never did he raise his voice, and seldom did I see him annoyed or put out. He had a marvellous sense of humour, and was not beyond playing a practical joke. Granville was the butt of what I should think is one of the oldest gags in creation; a gag that has been worked in every walk of life one way or another. It was one of those days when nothing would go right for Granny, and for some unknown reason he was muffing his lines. In take after take he would trip up over one line or another until he became something in the nature of a nervous wreck. Victor was the personification of patience, soothing him, encouraging him, urging him on. Practically the whole day had gone on this one scene. Then, about a quarter to six in the evening we started on another. It was a long scene, running some five to six minutes and using a fairly considerable amount of film. Granny went through it perfectly. Victor was delighted, and said so and had just started to say that would do for the day, that we would just go and see the rushes of the previous day's shooting and then go home, when he turned to the cameraman, Bill Skoll, and exclaimed in a loud voice:

"What! No . . . , but Bill, you should see that there *is* film in the camera before I give the word to shoot." Then turning to Granny, "Did you hear that? He says he forgot to reload the camera. There was no film in it."

There was a deathly silence, then something like a wail came from Granny. I really thought for a moment he was going to burst into tears. But before that could happen, Victor turned to Bill Skoll again with:

"Oh, you meant in your *own* cine-camera. Well, if Mr. Granville would like to go through it again especially for you . . ."

At this point he rose from his chair hurriedly and left the studio at a run, hotly pursued by Pooh-Bah brandishing Ko-Ko's axe.

I cannot let the opportunity pass of telling a story about our dog, Bisto, a wire terrier of a breed better known in the north of England than the south and a most friendly person. As his "doctor" always said: "He thinks everybody is on his side." He was extremely obedient, so far as we, his mistress and master were concerned, but should we ever permit him to go out with anyone else he would play them up no end. As a house dog we didn't think much of him. When we were with him in the house —wonderful. He would create enough noise to raise the neighbourhood. But when we returned to the house after leaving him alone for any length of time, not a sound. He would be waiting behind the front door with a look of extreme boredom on his face, coupled with a tinge of remonstrance, as much as to say: "This is a fine time to come home." Leave him in the car, and he would greet anyone entering it as a long-lost friend.

One day I was waiting in my dressing room for a call onto the set. It seemed to be a long time coming, so I thought I would go and see how things were progressing, get some idea of how much more time I would have, and then perhaps go and have a coffee. I could not have judged things better, and within two minutes I was shooting. During the take Victor Schertzinger wanted a certain assistant director, but he wasn't there, nor could he be found, nor was he found until shooting was over for the day and I returned to my dressing room. My wife had gone into town for the day and I had been keeping Bisto in my room. As I opened the door, there on the settee was our assistant director playing with him. I was a bit surprised and asked him how long he'd been there, as there had been a bit of a flap about him.

"Thank heaven you've come," he said. "I can't get out."

"But the door wasn't locked," I told him.

"No, I know it isn't," he returned. "I came to call you to the set. I knocked, but there was no reply, so I tried the door. It was open and I came in, intending to see if you were in your bathroom. The dog was standing in the middle of the room, and seemed quite pleased to see me. Brought me his bone, let me scratch his ear. I went on in, but you weren't there, so I made to go out. Quick as lightning Bisto got between me and the door, bared his teeth, and growled like mad. Oh, I've been all right—so long as I played "bones" with him and didn't attempt to leave. He won't let me out."

I burst out laughing—but it was a revelation. I don't know who taught the dog—but there was no doubt about it, he was a good house dog.

I let the assistant director out myself, and nobody could have been nicer than Bisto was as he wagged a cheery tail in farewell.

❊❊❊❊❊❊❊❊❊❊❊❊❊❊❊❊❊❊❊❊

TWELVE

Smoke but No Fire

Altogether, we were close on ten weeks on the picture, working right through what would otherwise have been my normal vacation. The company was due to pay a third visit to the United States, crossing probably towards the end of August or the beginning of September, but the Munich crisis put a stop to that.

We were in Stratford-on-Avon when that historical meeting took place. I seem to remember its being a Saturday with the inevitable matinee. We had a fairly good house, but it was obvious that very few of either the audience or the cast had their minds on *The Mikado*. I was sharing a room in the theatre with Granny, and the gloom was thick enough to dim the lights. In an effort to cheer myself up I repeatedly sang a version of *It Ain't Gonna Rain No More*—my words being *There Ain't Gonna Be No War*.

As everybody knows there was no war—for another twelve months. The news that it had been averted came through with the evening papers, and the effect on our audience was apparent at once. In fact, our reception seemed to me to be tinged with hysteria while retaining the fear of "What will Hitler do now?"

There was another near panic in Stratford that week in the

Without Make-up

Lance Corporal William Martyn Green, 1916

Myself, My Father, and My Brother Alex, 1908

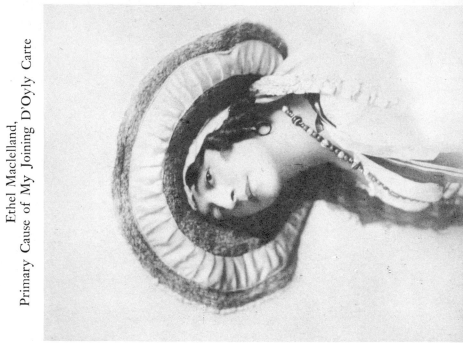

Ethel Maclelland,
Primary Cause of My Joining D'Oyly Carte

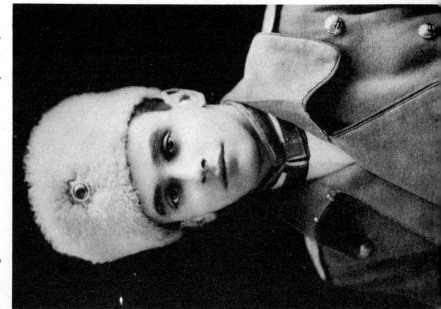

As Capt. Paul Petrov
in George Edwardes' Production of *Sybil*, 1921–22

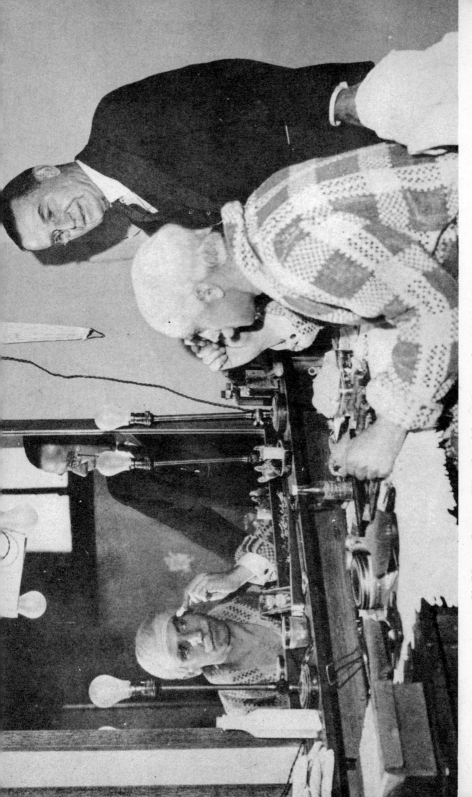

Sir Henry Lytton Watches Me Make Up for Major-General Stanley

14

"Oh! a private buffoon is a light-hearted loon."

Two Jack Points: Sir Henry Lytton and Self

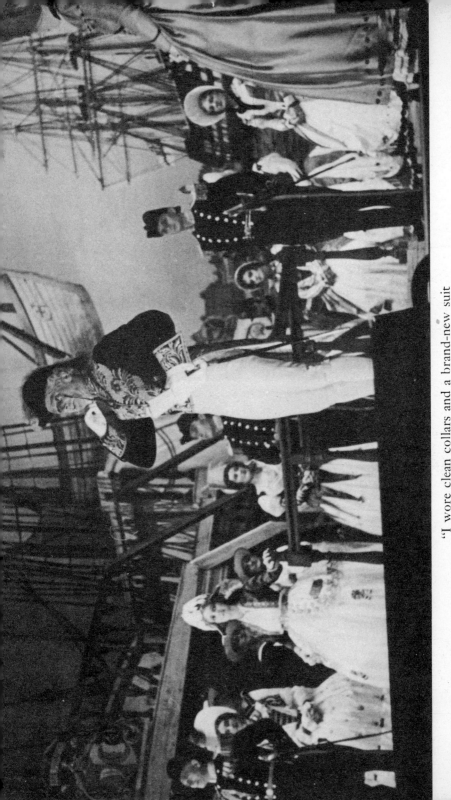

"I wore clean collars and a brand-new suit
For the pass examination at the Institute."

As Sir Joseph Porter in *H.M.S. Pinafore*

As Robin Oakapple in *Ruddigore*

Youth and Age

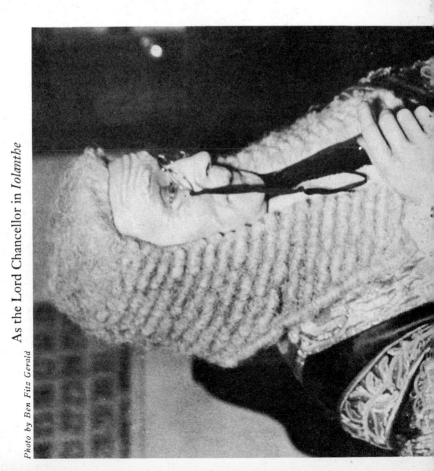

As the Lord Chancellor in *Iolanthe*

Photo by Ben Fitz Gerald

"I've an irritating chuckle, I've a celebrated sneer."

As King Gama in *Princess Ida*

"I am so proud . . ."

Sydney Granville as Pooh-Bah, Self as Ko-Ko, Gregory Stroud as Pish-Tush

Filming *The Mikado*

"Let me marry Yum-Yum tomorrow, and in a month you may behead me."
Self as Ko-Ko, Kenny Baker as Nanki-Poo

"Oh, Hollow! Hollow! Hollow!"

As Bunthorne in *Patience*

"Then Frederic, let your escort lion-hearted
Be summoned to receive a General's blessing."

Self as Major-General Stanley, John Dean as Frederic in *The Pirates of Penzance*

The Duke of Plaza-Toro Touches Up His Wig

John Dean as Box, Self as Cox

Menu by James Montgomery Flagg for Lotos Club Dinner

As the Lord Chancellor

An Oil Painting by James Montgomery Flagg

Farewell Party at Florentine Gardens, Hollywood

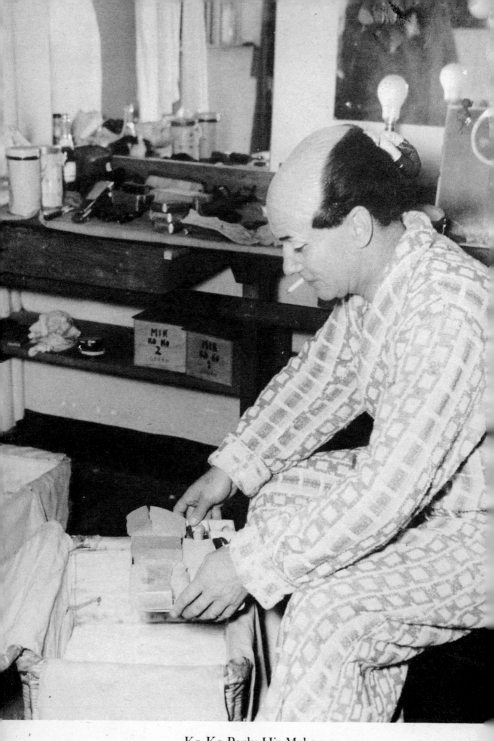

Ko-Ko Packs His Make-up

theatre itself. Someone had most carelessly thrown a cigarette away without looking to see where the burning end went—and it went into a basket containing the supers' costumes for *The Yeomen*. Soon it began to smoulder and set off clouds of smoke that seeped up through the stage and through to the auditorium. We were playing *Patience* that night, and the smoke first became evident just as we entered on the finale of the first act. Long before the curtain came down both stage and auditorium were thick with it. Isidore Godfrey became a mere wraith, and it was very clear that the audience were becoming quite restless.

The show carried on, though how much could be seen by those in front is problematical. But the fact that it did carry on undoubtedly averted a panic in the first instance, and, before the curtain had completely descended, Mr. Tossell, the theatre's resident manager, was on the stage in front of it, where he completed the panic-saving by assuring everyone that there was absolutely no danger. His opening words brought the laugh of the evening: "You may possibly have noticed some smoke."

It really was very nearly a true case of smoke without fire. Certainly there were no flames, but the materials of the costumes had smouldered completely away to the accompaniment of clouds of smoke. To clear this away it was decided to open the sliding roof of the theatre—the fire having been put out by the fire brigade—and quite shortly the theatre began to resume its normal state of visibility. It was a warmish night, so there was no hurry to close the roof, and no attempt was made to do so until just before Leslie Rands and I started on our last duet, "When I go out of door."

I was no more than halfway through the first verse when there came a deep rumbling followed by a report like a cannon and a rain of large pieces of cast iron. Odd pieces flew past my ears into the orchestra pit, others bounced around my feet. I saw Leslie Rands go off the stage hurriedly, and it crossed my mind that he had been hit with a lump. Bits were still falling— I was still singing, and the only thing that worried me was whether I could remember Leslie's lines and at the same time readapt them to myself and thus keep the show going. I heaved a great sigh of relief when I saw Leslie return to the stage and carry on. He had been struck a glancing blow with a fair-sized lump and like a wise man had sought refuge in the wings until the avalanche had ceased. During his verse I had time to look around and see a quantity of the pieces that had fallen, and the size of them, and I realized what a very narrow escape we had both had.

It was the first time the roof had been opened since its instal-lation. It had grown a little stiff, and the extra power needed to operate it found the flaws in the cast-iron crank wheel, so that the whole thing had collapsed in pieces. Several of the orchestra had near misses, and it is amazing that none of the instruments were touched. It also dawned on me that had it occurred but two or three minutes later the whole company would have been on the stage and casualties would have been inevitable. I think we were nearer to a panic then than at the thickest of the smoke. Following on the recent war scare I am convinced that half the audience thought that Hitler had attacked without warning— though why he should have chosen the Stratford Memorial Theatre as his first objective I've yet to find out.

We did eventually sail for America on our third visit on Christmas Eve, 1938, opening once again at the Martin Beck Theatre, on January 5, 1939. This was our shortest visit to date and included only Philadelphia and Boston on our itinerary fol-lowing the New York season.

Although the New York season was practically half over when we arrived, theatreland was still busy, and several old friends were appearing on Broadway, among them Conway Tearle, whom I had first met in Philadelphia in 1935, and Maurice Evans. Walter Huston had just finished a run with Maxwell Anderson and Kurt Weill's *Knickerbocker Holiday* —and that was something of an old friend, too, for I can claim some sort of indirect credit for his magnificent success in the role of Peter Stuyvesant, the last governor of New Netherland. I had been approached through Richard Bird to play the part; but when Bird reached me, I had unfortunately, just two hours previously, signed a contract with Carte, tying me up until the middle of 1942.

They made efforts to get Carte to release me, but he refused. That apparently put them in a spot, as it seems that Maxwell had more or less written the part with me in mind. They knew they could do nothing about it, but asked whether I could suggest somebody. To this day I don't know what made me choose the name I did, but I mentioned Walter Huston. When I saw him in the role later on in Philadelphia, I told him that I was glad I had been unable to accept the role in the first instance. Had I done so it would have robbed me of the pleasure of witnessing his performance and hearing him sing that delightful and appealing song, "The September Song." That was no flattery— I meant every word, and I still do. He was magnificent in the part; and his singing of that song was brilliant and masterly.

John Barrymore was also in town. I did a broadcast with him, and to my intense surprise was given permission to sing two songs out of the G. & S. operas—"Titwillow," and "John Wellington Wells" from *The Sorcerer*. Actually, G. & S. is in the

public domain in the United States. The story of how that came
about has been told elsewhere, so I do not propose to tell it here.
I mention the fact only because if it had been anyone but myself doing this broadcast it would not have been necessary to
obtain permission. But I, being a member of the D'Oyly Carte
and so an employee of Rupert of that name, was restricted to
the theatres where his company was being presented, unless I
obtained special dispensation direct from him. He had been
known to give similar permission twice before: once to allow
Derek Oldham, Sylvia Cecil, and myself to appear on a programme with Alexander Woollcott. I regret to say that I do
not recall the details of his programme that evening other than
that he dealt at some length on the subject of the Seeing Eye,
and that at one point he "serenaded," with our assistance, an
elderly lady who was a great lover of the operas, and, if my
memory does not completely desert me, was closely connected
with the Seeing Eye movement.

The other occasion on which permission was given was for
a programme that went by the title of "The Magic Hour"—a
Sunday night programme. Once again it was Derek Oldham,
Sylvia Cecil, and myself. What the main purpose of the programme was, other than entertainment, I do not know. I know
we were all three spending a week-end with friends on Long
Island and had to cut our visit short in order to make the broadcast.

But in spite of the precedent set by the two occasions, I was
still surprised that I received the permission I did. Granted it
was a Sunday night programme, granted, too, that it was an
unsponsored programme, still that was by virtue of the fact that
the broadcasting company sending it out was doing so only in
the hopes of selling it to a sponsor. However, I got the necessary

permit, duly sang, and at the same time renewed my acquaintance with John.

My wife had never met him and thought she would be interested to do so; so a little later on in the season I asked him to lunch with us at Sardi's—with his wife, of course. He had not long been married to his "current wife," as he himself put it. A date was fixed and the time, one o'clock, settled. My wife and I were there waiting, the table was booked. By fifteen minutes past Jack had not arrived and I was beginning to think that he had probably forgotten all about it when a phone message came through. No apology. Just a bare statement that he was just getting into a taxi and would be there in ten minutes.

So far as I knew, nobody was aware that Jack was lunching either with me or at Sardi's, but obviously whoever received the message had spread the good news round and within three minutes there was a mass of people round the entrance waiting for him. A taxi drew up, and out jumped Jack, followed by two women, one quite young and the other quite a deal older. Jack stalked down the restaurant to our table, stopped, and said: "Martyn, I'm sorry I'm late." I introduced him to my wife. He drew the younger of the two women forward:

"Martyn—Mrs. Green, this is my wife, Elaine." Then he brought the other forward. "My wife's mother—she would come."

Lunch was a riot.

Renee Carroll, the red-headed hat check girl at Sardi's, is probably one of the best-known personalities in New York. She has an amazing memory. Once she knows you—or, I should say, once she decides to know you—she never gives you a check for your hat and coat. I don't know how many people she attends to in the course of one lunchtime, but it must be considerable, and the majority, being more or less regular customers and "known," do not receive any check. She just takes the hat, and coat if there is one, greets one by name, and moves on to the next person. Never once has she made a mistake when handing back as you leave. A few years ago she celebrated her, I think, twenty-first year there. As her patrons collected their hats on leaving, *she* presented *them* with a quarter.

Our general manager, Alfred Nightingale, went in one lunchtime shortly after he arrived to settle the final details of a forthcoming visit of the company to New York. As he handed his hat to Renee he told her:

"An old friend of yours will be returning soon—Martyn Green."

"Ahh," exclaimed she, "he's just a hat to me."

So much for fame.

I have not forgotten, though, that during the last war—in 1943—I was on my way back to England from California via New York. Not wishing to let tradition go completely I repaired to Sardi's for my first meal in the city. I was in R.A.F. uniform, and it had been a matter of four years since I had last set foot in the place. Renee was there, as usual. I handed over my greatcoat and cap. She took it, but there was no glimmer of recognition on her face, and I said nothing for a moment. When she turned to another customer without having given me a check I asked her, "Don't I get a ticket or something?" Like a flash her answer came back: "Since when did you ever get a ticket, Mr. Green? Or do I have to call you Captain now?"

She was not the only one to remember me, in spite of my uniform. I had a few moments to wait for my two guests and moved into the small foyer just beside the cocktail bar. Two seconds later the bartender was in front of me with a tray and my usual cocktail.

"I didn't order that," I told him.

"But it's what you always have, Mr. Green—" and then, inevitably, "or is it Captain now?"

And "Captain" it had to be. "Flight Lieutenant" was just a little too much.

It was about this time that F.P.A. (Franklin P. Adams) showed me a cutting from the *New York Sun* with a story in it that I think will bear repeating. I say I "think" it was about this time, but it is now so long ago, and I have unfortunately lost the cutting itself and so cannot check on the date, that it could very well have been two years earlier. I haven't forgotten the story, though, and here it is:

A certain journalist of the drama critic order was not averse in any way to the pleasures of alcohol—indeed, he had at times been known to indulge to an extent that was far from wise, and when in that condition given to raising his voice in song. On more than one occasion he had been "picked up" for singing in the public highway at an hour (2 to 3 A.M.) in a manner calculated to create a nuisance. One night he was picked up in Washington Square and haled to the nearest precinct or police station, and a charge was preferred. Asked if he had anything to say, he informed them that he had been celebrating the return of some very good friends from England—to wit, The DeeOily Carty Opera Troupe. They had opened that night and he'd been along to see them. He liked Gilbert and Sullivan and had felt so good about the whole thing that as soon as he'd got his column written and sent in he'd gone off to have a drink in celebration. If he had been a nuisance, he was sorry, but there it was. Whoever was in charge was also a great lover of the operas, and that fact tempered justice with more than mercy. After agreeing that the occasion was one to be celebrated he released the offender with the final admonition:

". . . but see to it that it doesn't happen again. This is your last chance. If you're brought into this stationhouse again you're in for it."

He was duly, if somewhat thickly, thanked, and our journalistic friend turned and weaved his way out of the building. The last that was seen and heard of him, he was tripping blithely down the steps of the stationhouse singing lustily:

"Taken from the county jail,
By a set of curious chances . . ."

They are queer people, dramatic critics. During one of our visits it struck me that the critics of New York were not so much criticising the various shows as they came along—and that season there were many—as trying to write a funnier and wittier column than their rivals of the other papers. There was hardly a show that was not panned or that did not at least feel their caustic and cruel wit. I won't say that all the critics behaved in that way. Brooks Atkinson, I'm sure, cruel though he may be, would not be that way just for the sake of raising a cheap laugh from his readers at the expense of either the show or any one of the performers. We of the D'Oyly Carte did not escape. Full many a show failed to secure a run almost entirely due to the extremely adverse reports given them by this peculiarity of the majority of the critics.

Some of the notices were very amusing, though, I must admit. Quite frequently in the same paper one would see widely varying opinions. As far back as 1934 F.P.A. said, in the November issue of *Stage* in New York, under the title "First Night Thoughts": "These first nights (of each of the operas) at the

Martin Beck have . . . brought to New York the atmosphere of a small town with its stock (repertory) company and its favorites . . . I don't see why, though I'm anything but clever, they don't play New York for ever!"

In the same issue Samuel Chotzinoff of the *Post* is quoted as having said in his review: "*The Mikado,* though first-rate Sullivan, is only second-rate Gilbert." Going back many years to one of our very much earlier tours—the 1929 tour, I believe it was—Sir Henry Lytton was the target. They said of him—and he was fond of repeating this story against himself—"If Henry Lytton, the alleged comedian, is funny, then a funeral's a scream."

If Henry could tell one against himself, I'm sure I can. I quote from two criticisms of myself in New York: ". . . I'm not quite sure whether I was seeing Olsen and Johnson in *The Mikado,* or Martyn Green in *Hellzapoppin'* "—which, now I look at it, and knowing who and what Olsen and Johnson were, could be taken as a compliment—though I doubt it was meant that way. I quote again: "Martyn Green thinks he's funny. He not only thinks he's funny, he all but comes down into the auditorium with a plate handing out little notices to tell us he is."

Two excerpts from criticisms of other plays that are without a doubt witty, but—: Of the play *Alley Cat,* Stephen Rathbun of the *New York Sun* said: "In the third act Jean tries unsuccessfully to commit suicide by inhaling gas, but is saved by the doctor. The Consolidated Gas Company should be notified about the poor flow of gas." And Percy Hammond of the *Herald Tribune* said, of *Divided by Three:* "You will admire *Divided by Three* as you might a beautiful wig, while fearful that at any moment it might come off."

However, all the critics may be bad some of the time, and some of the critics all of the time, but they can't all be bad all of the time, and for that I am grateful, for on the whole they have all been good to me, most of the time, and when they weren't—well, maybe I deserved it, and when they were constructive while yet damning, I hope I took notice and acted upon their advice.

As you can see, I am of two minds about drama critics! I am also sometimes of two minds about American hospitality. I have already said enough to show how grateful I am for the kindnesses I have met at every turn. But sometimes there has been more than a dash of bitter with the sweet. All want to show you a "good time," and nearly all succeed. One can never complain that their desire to do so is anything but sincere, but sometimes their method of doing so is little more than cruel and certainly overpowering.

To give an example, I had for some weeks been pestered, and I use the word unreservedly, to spend a Sunday with some people on Long Island. Time after time I found some excuse to refuse until they put the date so far ahead (and incidentally told me that Derek Oldham had already accepted, a statement that was not in strict accordance with the truth, as I discovered later, for Derek had only said, "I'll see") that I had to accept.

It was arranged that some friends of theirs—I mention no names, for obvious reasons—should pick us up at our apartment at ten in the morning. This they did and we were driven out, arriving at the appointed rendezvous—a certain yacht club— in time for lunch at twelve-thirty. The lunch was very good, and I began to think that after all, perhaps, I had been mistaken in my original estimation of them. The afternoon was spent in looking around the place, and by four-thirty both my wife and

I were dying for that panacea for all ills, a cup of tea. But none was forthcoming. Then I was asked if I minded going to their home. There would be a meal, and their children, of course, and just one or two people they had invited in to meet me. I didn't mind, did I? There was little I could do under the circumstances but accept.

Arriving at their home, I was shown the geography of the house and retired to clean up. On my return the living room, empty when I had retired some ten minutes previously, was full. I got the impression that every child in the neighbourhood had been brought in with their fathers and mothers, sisters, cousins, and aunts. I was given a plate with some food on it, which I took in one hand, and a cup of coffee, which I took in the other.

If there was one thing I really did want then, it was a drink. I don't think I am anything like a heavy drinker, but I do like my "tot" and I do like my cocktail, neither of which I had had all day long. Nor did I get one then. To make it worse, I found myself surrounded by these hordes of children and masses of adults. I was then sung at by the children, who gave me everything they had ever learned, and I was sung at by the fathers, who formed themselves into a sort of glee party and gave me everything from the complete contents of the *Yale Songbook* to the full repertoire of the Gilbert and Sullivan operas.

I was still holding my plate with some food on it in one hand, and the coffee—stone cold—in the other. I was questioned on this opera, that opera, this performer and that performer. Suddenly I heard a voice, a woman's voice (not my wife's—she was going through a similar catechism in a slightly smaller way). The voice said:

"Mr. Green, if you have to be back in town for that rehearsal at nine o'clock I think you had better be on your way."

The voice, I discovered, belonged to the wife of the man who had driven us out in the morning. My coffee cup and plate were removed from my hands, my hat and coat were thrust into them. I vaguely remember making my farewells and being led out to the car, where I was put into the back with my wife on one side and the voice on the other. We moved off.

A few minutes later, without saying a word, our rescuer pulled a tray down behind the back seat, revealing a sort of cupboard. Reaching into this, she pulled out a cocktail shaker and glasses. Filling one, she handed it to me, and then one to my wife. When they were empty she refilled them and then proceeded to lay out a most delicious meal. Cold turkey, salad, shrimp cocktails, sweets, and dessert. Still without saying a word she helped us both to food and drink—strong hot coffee, and finally, brandy. When I'd finished, feeling a much stronger and fitter person than when I'd entered the car, I turned and said:

"What made you say that I had a rehearsal to-night? I haven't. We never rehearse on a Sunday."

"I know," she said, "but I saw that glassy stare and fixed smile of the mentally overpowered and thought it was time I rescued you."

"But this meal, and the drinks!" I asked, amazedly. "Where—how—?"

"I had a vague suspicion that it would turn out as it did, so—we came prepared. And don't thank me, it's not necessary."

But we did—profusely. They dropped us off at our apartment somewhere around ten o'clock, having driven slowly to allow us to eat in comfort—and that, I'm sorry to say, is the last time I saw them.

Yes, American hospitality is amazing.

THIRTEEN

Some Sort of Celebration

The month of May, 1939, saw us back in England for a sea-
son at Sadler's Wells. That season concluded, my wife and I
went to Norway for our first vacation in two years; but we
had to be back in London in August, a full week before we
opened the new tour at Bournemouth, in order to have some
fittings for the new Jack Point costumes in the redesigned *Yeo-*
men of the Guard. Rupert Carte had been toying with the idea
of "something new" for some time and eventually approached
Peter Goffin for new "sets" and new costumes.

Many will, of course, have seen this new setting by now—in
fact it is quite probable that the old scenery and costumes will
hardly be remembered by a large number of the patrons of
G. & S.—so there is little need for me to describe it. Some people
like it, some have hailed it as brilliant, while others have con-
demned it utterly. The principal idea underlying Peter Goffin's
design was to get away from the overpowering mass of dark
and dismal reproduction of the whole of the Tower of London
and an action that took place on a completely flat stage, and to
avoid dressing the "Citizens"—as opposed to the uniformed
Yeomen—in a series of similar clothes. As he told me: "I am

sure that even in those days the citizens of London didn't all dress alike."

The result of all this planning and designing was a shifting of the emphasis from the scenery, due to its simplified form, to the players themselves. A very laudable intention, one to be commended; but I still think that it was not necessary to simplify and modernize it to the extent of creating a Tower of London in pink concrete. Nor including a rather grotesque woodcut for a tree. Perhaps after all I am still a realist, so far as scenery for the *Yeomen of the Guard* goes anyway.

As for the costumes, well! My first act was not too bad, and had undoubteldy been well thought out. Jack Point, as was pointed out, was "out of work," and it is hardly to be expected that he would be permitted to keep his uniform on leaving his last job. He would be wearing whatever manner of clothing he had been lucky enough to beg, borrow, steal, or have thrown at him by his master as being worn out or of no further use. Hence the rather mixed costume worn in that first act. But the second act was a costume that never, I am convinced, graced any English jester at any time. I always had the impression that the design was taken straight from a print of Grimaldi. I did not like it, and I doubt I ever will.

I begged, appealed, implored, and argued with Rupert and Peter (I always argued with Peter—he says "fought"—and I imagine I always will if he is designing costumes for me) to change the costume. I even went to the British Museum and made some crude sketches of all the authentic Jester costumes I could find (there was ne'er a one that corresponded in the slightest degree to Peter's). But all to no avail. I played my trump card—not that it was intended as a trump card; I was practically weeping with rage and frustration. They—he—Mr.

Carte had better get someone else to play the part. I didn't like the costume, never would, and feeling that way didn't think I would be able to give anything like a performance wearing it. Carte smiled quietly, "I think you'll do very well. Once you are on the stage in it, you'll forget it," he said.

We were to open in Bournemouth the first week in September. *Yeomen of the Guard* was not included in the programme for that week. The following Sunday we listened to Chamberlain's declaration of war against Germany. It looked as if my statement that I could not play the part of Point in that costume would now read "would not," as that was my last appearance with the D'Oyly Carte Opera Company until 1946.

When we awoke on that fateful Friday morning to the news that Poland had been invaded, the shock was terrific. That war was inevitable was a foregone conclusion. Bournemouth was transformed in a matter of minutes almost from a happy—I won't say carefree—holiday resort to a town of solemn-faced, speculating, wondering people—wondering how soon they could, and *if* they would, get home. We of the company were wondering, if war came (the "if" being the hope, doomed though it may be, that springs eternal in the human breast), what would happen to the tour. Would we open at Southsea the next week or not? The government had already made a statement to the effect that all theatres and places of entertainment where numbers of people congregated at one time would automatically be closed. Their reopening would depend on how the situation developed. (In actual fact, theatres were beginning to operate again within two to three weeks.)

My wife and I decided that in any case we would go up to Stratford-on-Avon to our good friends Cran and Watney, the proprietors of the Arden Hotel, where we always stayed when there. It was on the road between Bournemouth and Stratford, in a small wayside pub, that we heard Chamberlain tell the nation that we were at war as from eleven o'clock that morning. When Chamberlain finished speaking, we all looked at each other blankly for a moment or two. There were five of us all together; ourselves, the landlord, and another couple who had pulled up behind us as we knocked on the pub door to see if we might listen to the broadcast. The landlord was the first to speak:

"Well," he said, "I think that calls for some sort of celebration."

"Celebration?" We all echoed, amazed at his choice of word in the face of such grave news—but nevertheless feeling that his idea, whatever the word used, was the right one.

"Yes," said the landlord, "celebration. We are going to celebrate the beginning of the end of Herr Bloody Hitler and Co. If he can start a war out of hours on a Sunday then we can drink to his roasting in Hades at the same time."

And we did.

It was a queer sensation, driving into London that evening. We seemed to be the only people going in that direction. And everyone in the streams of traffic that passed in the opposite direction appeared to regard us as if we were totally mad.

On the Monday morning, after a night that brought us our first air-raid warning—which proved to be a false alarm, but was nevertheless extremely disconcerting, for after all it was our first—I went up to the offices at the Savoy to find out about the Southsea visit. It was off. That was no surprise. I asked Dicky Collett what he thought was going to happen, and as I came within the "call-up" ages, as published by the government, what would my position be? He told me that he thought the present situation as regarded the theatres would probably last about a fortnight. As he pointed out, entertainment was going to prove a very necessary thing. By closing the theatres for too long they would be depriving the public of a very great contribution towards the upkeep of morale. As for myself, I needn't worry. Mr. Carte would be taking the necessary steps very shortly to ensure that I would be "screened." And in any case it was most unlikely that men of my age group would be called for some time—if at all. The best thing I could do would be to take it easy, and be ready to carry on with the tour at any moment.

On the Wednesday, just two mornings later, I received a letter from Mr. Carte informing me that, in view of the government's order closing all theatres, he considered it necessary to suspend the rest of the tour. If the government were to allow theatres to reopen at a later date, *and it was practicable for him to re-form the company*, he would be only too glad to offer me a *fresh engagement if my services were available.*

I was under contract with him for the run of that tour, with options on his part, should he care to exercise them, until 1942. I assumed, rightly, as it turned out, that his letter really meant that he was invoking a war clause in the contract and terminating the contract and with it any options he might have.

I saw Dicky again and asked him if he had any ideas as to when the company would be re-formed, to which he replied that he had no idea at all. He was as much surprised and as much in the dark as I, for he was in the same boat. His contract as general manager of the D'Oyly Carte Opera Company had been terminated. As he was still on the Board of Directors of the Savoy Hotel, though, he maintained his office there. But not only he was in the same boat; Miss Dawe, and Miss Darly, secretary to the company of twenty-five years' standing and stenographer of eighteen years' standing respectively, were also, putting it bluntly, sacked.

In view of all that, his letter to me was far too nebulous a thing to place any great degree of hope in, so I promptly went round to see an agent who had approached me more than once. Within twenty-four hours I had signed a contract with C. B. Cochran to co-star in a revue with Evelyn Laye and Clifford Mollison, with Doris Hare, Phyllis Stanley, and James Hayter in the cast. We went into rehearsal towards the end of October and opened in Manchester at the opera house for a four-week season terminating just before Christmas, when we went on to Glasgow for another four. This was, of course, the usual try-out before going to London, and included three weeks in Edinburgh.

One story I must tell before I go any further. When we were in Glasgow, Sir Harry Lauder was in to see the show and came backstage afterwards to see us all. He said he had enjoyed it quite well; in fact, ". . . it was no sae bad, and quite wurr-rr-th the money Ah paid tae see it." Cocky had presented him with a box.

The theatres opening once again, Dicky Collett had got busy on Carte and, by dint of much pressure, induced Carte to re-form. I, of course, was not available and was not even approached in the matter of an engagement. Dicky re-assumed his position as general manager, and most of the members of the company were re-engaged. Miss Dawe and Miss Darly did not take up their jobs again. The company opened in Edinburgh a week after we went to Glasgow, and rather ironically, exchanged theatres with us when we went to Edinburgh.

It came to my ears later, quite a bit later, that Carte had suggested that I had "let the company down"—apparently by not being available!

Following the three weeks in Edinburgh, *Lights Up*—the title by which the revue was known—was due to open, again ironically, at the Savoy Theatre on February 6, 1940. The main body of the company went to London on the Sunday morning, but "Boo" Laye, Doris Hare, Phyllis Stanley, Clifford Mollison, and myself took off from Turnhouse Aerodrome at 9 A.M. for Kirkwall, where we changed planes and flew over to Hoy, Scapa Flow. Boo had met the admiral in command during the early part of our Edinburgh visit and suggested that some of us would like to go up to Scapa and give the boys there a bit of a concert—something they just didn't get, as Scapa was not an "open" area. Admiral Lister jumped at the offer, pulled several strings, overcame the difficulties of the order forbidding non-Service personnel to enter the area, arranged the flight with the Scottish Airways, by permission of the Air Ministry, and met us, the first civilians to set foot on the island of Hoy, the main naval base at Scapa Flow, as we stepped out of the plane.

We gave a concert that lasted close on three hours, with excerpts from our show as well as individual turns. We were helped out with one turn who was not a member of the *Lights Up* party, a chief petty officer who put on a really excellent conjuring act. I learned from him shortly after he came off that he had been a steward, I think he said chief saloon steward, on the royal yacht, and it had frequently fallen to his lot to keep the young princes entertained with his tricks. But what a joy those boys were to entertain! They were wonderful.

After the concert the Admiral addressed them and proposed a vote of thanks to the performers, ". . . these good people who have given up their Sunday to fly here just to entertain you," he said. I had to smile. *We* had given up our *Sunday*. For all the world as if they hadn't given up, not just a Sunday, but every other day of the week as well, and not only for one week, either, in order to keep a navy ready to fight. They cheered us to the echo—and I felt slightly embarrassed. But our visit did one thing. It started something that ENSA carried on with, and soon party after party went up to entertain.

We had to stay overnight on the island, taking off the next morning at 6 A.M., changing planes once more at Kirkwall. It was glorious when we left Kirkwall, but gradually the ceiling got lower and lower. We had some hills to go over, but our pilot did not care to take the risk of going over in the thick cloud, so down we came to look for a landing. An aerodrome was spotted and we made for it. By this time, "even the sparrows were walking," and it was high time we were on the ground ourselves. The aerodrome chosen happened to be Leuchars, an R.A.F. station. As we taxied to a standstill, Service cars streamed out to us. They had had no information that we were coming in, or that anyone was coming in for that matter, and naturally a somewhat belligerent curiosity was aroused. After the pilot I was the first out of the plane. Both of us were surrounded and "Who are you? Why have you come in here? What do you want? What's the idea?" was shot at us from, I presumed, the Adjutant and the Flying Control Officer. I began to say something about being a theatrical party coming down from Scapa.

"What theatrical party? We know nothing about any theatrical party." I felt at the moment that I was in imminent danger of arrest as a spy. I hurriedly mentioned the name of Evelyn

Laye. As I spoke she came out of the plane, and I quickly introduced her. The effect was electrical.

We left there by Service cars after a magnificent lunch at somewhere about three in the afternoon. The plane was grounded for the night due to fog, and we finished our journey by train, catching the sleeper for London at ten that night and arriving there just in time to snatch a hurried breakfast and dash off to a rehearsal for a broadcast of one or two excerpts of the show.

During rehearsals several of us went out to Epsom to give a concert to the troops there. Boo and I had a number in the show that we thought we would like to "try out on the dog," and this concert was just the opportunity we were looking for. The number in question involved a short dance from me and a final exit with both of us dancing off, Boo leading. The number itself was a great success, but the final exit was a riot. The stage on which we were performing was of necessity a homemade affair erected by the troops themselves under the Epsom Racecourse grandstand. It consisted of a series of planks set on trestles, and a proscenium of bunting draped round a somewhat flimsy skeleton framework. We made our exit to the right, Boo about two paces ahead of me. She was all right—heaven knows how—but I, I suppose, must have taken a step more than she—and instead of a stage on which to set down my foot there was just a void, which I couldn't see owing to its being hidden by the bunting, and down I went, bringing with me half the stage.

F O U R T E E N

Marking Time

Our opening at the Savoy with Lights Up *was, I imagine, the* last of the "big" openings for many years—practically a fully "dressed" audience. What a pity it is that the custom of dressing for the theatre has become almost non-existent! I, personally, am convinced that a "dressed" audience has a psychological effect on the players and results in a brighter performance. That is not snobbery, it is something I have, I think, proved through the years. It is not that you get a better performance, just that the performance is brighter. And quite probably it is the psychological effect of being dressed themselves—the audience, I mean—putting them into a gala mood, so to speak, that brings this about.

The fact remains, though, that once inside the theatre the blackout was forgotten and the war less than a dream. I went over to the Savoy Grill for supper with my wife, mother, and sisters after the performance. As we went in I noticed Rupert D'Oyly Carte seated at his usual table just to the right of the door. I thought our eyes had met and so smiled a "Good evening" to him. Obviously he could not have been looking at me at all, for he turned his head away without any sign of recognition.

We did not, I am afraid, run very long—three months, I think. It was not entirely the fault of the show, or of the people in it. A gradual worsening of the war situation, culminating in the invasion of Norway, was too much, so we closed and went on tour, finally closing down in May.

The late James Agate, incidentally, gave me what I think is one of the nicest and most complimentary notices I have ever had when he "wrote up" this revue. After giving his impressions of the show as a whole he discussed each of the performers in turn—Evelyn Laye, Clifford Mollison, Doris Hare, Phyllis Stanley, Gerald Nodin, and the rest—by which time *my* ego was feeling extremely deflated, as he had not mentioned me at all. There was still a bit more to read, however, and there, in the very last paragraph he said, ". . . There were also a number of other people who kept coming on, both old and young. I could not make out who they were at first—but came to the conclusion they were all Martyn Green."

During the run at the Savoy we had a visit from our Scapa Flow friend, Admiral Lister, who was down in London for a while before he went off to Norway. Naturally, we didn't know at the time that he was going there. It was not until much, much later that I discovered that was where he had been. We all had supper in the Savoy after a performance. Just after one dance a naval officer approached the table and greeted the Admiral, and it was pretty evident that he had had a few drinks. Nevertheless, Lister introduced him to the table. He chatted for a moment or two and then went off to his own party. I heard one of our party tell the Admiral they were surprised at his allowing an inebriated officer to approach him in that way, especially "that one" (he had at one time achieved a certain notoriety through the same cause, inebriation). The Admiral said very quietly:

"We have been shipmates more than once. At the moment that officer is doing a great job in destroyers. They don't often get leave, and when they do, who's to blame them if they get a little tight? Certainly not I."

I always liked Admiral Lister.

Shortly after *Lights Up* I formed an act with Sylvia Cecil and set out on a tour of the variety halls. Our act followed Will Fyfe's at Liverpool, and one night Sylvia and I were waiting in the wings, together with our accompanist, for him to finish when his valet came onto the stage. He whispered to us that "they" were overhead—meaning enemy aircraft. I had heard no air-raid warning sirens and said so, adding that I thought he must be mistaken. At that moment Will came off the stage, and warning or no warning, the first of a number of bombs fell. Will remarked that he didn't think those people up there liked his act, but even so they could register their disapproval in a quieter manner. Shaken though I was, for the bomb was too near to disregard, I had to smile.

That remark of Will's was all that was required to straighten us up. After a few minutes the manager went onto the stage and asked those of the audience who wished to go to shelters to make their way out quietly; for those who wished to remain, he said, the show would continue. If the all clear had not gone by the end of the performance the actors on the bill would carry on and endeavour to entertain any members of the public who wished to remain. We were in the theatre until four o'clock. Some of us were preparing to go across to another threatre—we had run out of material, and an exchange of turns was taking place—when the all clear went, and so did we.

That night was the beginning of a series of raids on Liverpool, of which we saw three—two in the theatre and one that did not start until we were on our way back to our hotel. The first thing Will did was to go straight to his room and collect a bottle of Scotch and a bottle of brandy. On his return the lounges and public rooms were entirely deserted, everybody having gone to shelters below—the squash courts being quite a favourite. We ourselves were being urged, in fact almost ordered, to follow their example. But Will would have none of it. He found out where the female staff were sheltering—particularly the floor maids and kitchen maids—and off he went, dragging me with him, and for as long as the raid was in progress, he remained with them, joking, singing, giving them all a tot of Scotch or brandy. It appeared later that after that first night's raid he had heard that the girls were very nervous, and during our second long night in the theatre he had been going backwards and forwards from theatre to hotel, hotel to theatre, for the purpose of giving them some moral support.

Our variety tour lasted only seven weeks. The London blitz was well on its way by this time, and shows were closing down all over the place. Many acts appearing in and around London were on long contracts that, being made in wartime, did not contain a war clause. These acts had to be found a place elsewhere, with the result that acts without dates already booked well ahead were out of luck.

My next venture was with Billy Mayerl and George Clarke, that crazy zany who could do things on the stage with a small Austin Seven car that could scare the wits out of you and reduce you to hysterical laughter at the same time. We three, together with several others, tried to put on a show in Slough. Billy rented a hall, and we rehearsed and opened to a full house headed by the mayor. It was the only full house we had, and we closed two weeks later. My salary for the two weeks was £11: ten for the two weeks with Billy, and one for a concert we were engaged for at a Slough factory's annual works dinner and dance. I rather imagine that Billy was out of pocket—he had financed the show in the first place.

By this time I had an application in for a commission in the Navy, one for the Army, and two for the R.A.F. My first for the R.A.F. was turned down—I had applied for general duties. I was too old. My second was for administrative and special duties. One of my sponsors in my second application was A. P. Herbert. The qualifications he gave as being a fit person to sponsor me were: Member of Parliament; Barrister at Law; Author; Petty Officer, Royal Naval Volunteer Reserve (Thames Conservancy). As he wrote it, he said:

"And the next time I see you I suppose I'll have to stand to attention, salute, and call you 'sir.' "

I did not see him again until the day I donned my uniform for the first time. I changed into it at my club. When fully attired as a "Pilot Officer on Probation—R.A.F.V.R.," I went down into the bar to "wet the stripe," and was on the point of doing so when who should walk in but Alan P. Herbert—also in his uniform of a Petty Officer, R.N.V.R. (Thames Conservancy). He took one look.

"I knew it." he said. Then he sprang to attention. "Good morning, sir."

But he got away with the salute. We were inside a building —a private building—and in consequence he was not wearing his cap. After that, we both wetted the stripe. Forty-eight hours later I had reported to Junior Officers' Training School and my career as an officer in the R.A.F. (V.R.) had begun.

But before that I had gone out with an ENSA (Entertainments National Service Association) tour of *School for Husbands,* an amusing comedy that had provided a vehicle for Harold Huth a few years earlier. This tour was among the first of a new experiment that was being tried out for the entertainment of troops in the more outlying districts, and camps where there was no provision for entertainment by way of a regular stage.

In the first instance we carried our own stage, an extraordinarily ingenious affair that could be folded and carried inside the bus that transported the cast, costumes, and necessary lighting equipment at the same time. When erected it gave a floor space of something like 14′ × 14′. By the time the stage had been set with the necessary furniture, which included a settee, a couple or so chairs, two occasional tables, etc., there was little enough room for the cast to move around, and when the full cast was on the stage, a thing that fortunately occurred only about twice during the show, one had to be extremely careful not to knock something—one of the actors, actresses, or pieces of furniture or props—flying. In largish halls, such as mess halls, drill halls, or aerodromes, the space between the walls of the hall and the proscenium uprights was usually masked in with bunting.

This was the cause of some considerable amusement to the troops on one occasion. We were putting the show on for the usual one night—stage, furniture, props and cast having been brought by bus from our headquarters at Shrewsbury to where we returned each night after the show—in a mess hall. Our stage consisted of half a dozen or so trestle tables from the mess itself—and those of my readers who have had anything like intimate contact with a mess trestle table will know only too well that they are not particularly noted for their stability—and there were eight of us, not to mention the scenery, furniture, and props. The only dressing accommodation was to each side of this "stage," the bunting used to mask the space between walls and proscenium uprights also acting as a curtain behind which the actors could dress—the gentlemen to one side, ladies to the other.

At one point in the second act I was on the stage with Vernon Kelse. We had a scene together, and although it was an amusing scene, it did not seem to me to be as funny as the laughter from the audience would indicate. I then realized that the audience's eyes were not on either of us; they were all looking to their left and beyond the limits of the stage.

Vernon was beginning to wonder if he had completed his dressing and was taking surreptitious glances at himself to make sure, then gave me an enquiring look. I managed to indicate that so far as I could see he was all right, and the scene proceeded with the accompanying laughter rising in volume and finally coming to an end with a unanimous but disappointed and drawn-out "O-o-h!" A few minutes later the leading lady made an entrance wearing a full evening gown and was received with rapturous applause, as much to her surprise as to ours. It was not a first entrance, nor one that called for applause in any way. But she acknowledged it very charmingly and carried on.

When the curtain came down on that act one of the officers, the adjutant I imagine, came backstage with the request that extra bunting might be hung between the walls and stage on the ladies' side. The existing bunting had proved to be inadequate to preserve the privacy of their dressing room, and

Marion had unconsciously given the boys an unexpected strip-tease act while changing from a tweed costume to an evening gown. The disappointed "O-o-h!" had come at the moment when she had slipped the gown over her head.

We headquartered in Shrewsbury for four weeks, where I met several old friends who had evacuated their families there, and then moved on to North Wales. Pwllheli, and don't ask me how to pronounce that, found us giving our play to an OCTU. The first person I met just after I arrived was Jack Hawkins. I knew he was in the army somewhere, as I had been to a small farewell party he gave at the Savage Club just before he went off to join his unit of the Royal Welsh Regiment as a private. We arranged to meet after the show and have a drink at the hotel. It was getting on for 9:45 P.M. before I was ready and time, for Jack, was getting short, his deadline being 10 P.M. Fortunately we ran into one of the senior N.C.O.'s. Jack introduced me; I asked him to join us, which he did. At approximately two minutes to ten he addressed Jack:

"Now then, young Hawkins, don't forget the time."

Jack meekly rose, took a brief farewell and departed with a slightly wry smile. The Sergeant relaxed back in his chair and carried on leisurely drinking his beer with a rather superior smile on his face. He did explain, though, that all those boys had to be up and out on a day's exercise by 6 A.M. and it was essential that they got in a good night's rest. I asked:

"Don't you have to go on these exercises?"

"Oh, yes," he said, "but I'm different. I'm used to 'em."

He left me at one in the morning.

My paper calling me to Air Ministry for an interview came through a week later. I drove down to London from North Wales and had my interview the next morning. I don't remember much about it except that I was asked a lot of questions, the principal one appearing to be: Did I realize that my pay as an officer in the R.A.F. would only be eleven shillings and ninepence a day? Realizing that, did I still wish to go on with my application? Apparently I answered all questions correctly, as after being told to retire for a few moments I was recalled to the examiners' room and instructed to report to the Medical Department for examination.

Four weeks later, to the day, I received my papers informing me I had been granted a commission in the Royal Air Force Volunteer Reserve, Administrative and Special Duties Branch, as from 11th April, 1941, exactly a week from receiving the papers.

I reported to Loughborough College, where the Junior Officers' Initial Training Course was carried out, after a hectic week in London getting fitted out with uniform, etc., going down to Worthing to see my mother and up to St. Albans to see my wife, who was driving ambulances there, on Friday 11th April.

I found that I was following in some very illustrious company, theatrically speaking. B. C. Hilliam (Flotsam) had been through the school about five weeks before; Hugh Wakefield about three; and I very nearly received strong disciplinary action for hailing Patrick Waddington with a shout when I should have been standing rigidly to attention. My excuse that I knew him very well was most unacceptable to the warrant officer in charge of the parade. Five minutes later an N.C.O. came up to the W.O. with a message which was passed on in that same W.O.'s stentorian voice:

"Pilot Officer Martyn Green—fall out and report to the Commandant immediately." All of my companions in my

"Flight," our drill sergeant, the W.O., thought I was "on the carpet." As for myself, I had visions of being drummed out of the Service.

I fell out in the approved fashion—spring to attention, one pace forward, pause, and march off in quick time. The message-bearing N.C.O. piloted me to where the commandant was waiting. As soon as we were out of earshot I asked him if he had any idea of why I was wanted. His reply was a noncommittal "No, sir." Coming up to the C.O., I gave him a smashing salute and announced myself in the manner laid down in the drill manuals:

"Pilot Officer Martyn Green reporting, sir."

"Ah, yes—er—" he began, "—er—stand easy, Mr. Green. I—er—ahem—I was wondering whether you could do me a favour." My eyes popped. "The D'Oyly Carte Opera Company are in Nottingham this week and I'd like to take my wife on Saturday night, but I can't get any tickets. Do you think you could use your influence to get me a couple?" Talk about bribery and corruption! The only thing I couldn't settle in my mind was who was bribing who, and which was corrupting the other. I decided to forget that angle of it, though, and said I would do my best, letting him know as soon as I knew myself.

I rang Freddie Hobbs at the theatre that night and eventually managed to persuade him that it was Martyn Green speaking, and that I was in the R.A.F., and it seemed pretty essential I should have two seats for the C.O. for Saturday night. He thought that could be arranged. I informed the C.O., who thanked me for my trouble, saw the show, and sent for me again on the Monday morning to say how much he had enjoyed it. He was sorry not to be able to see me in the role, but if I made as good an officer as I had a First Lord of the Admiralty then the R.A.F. would have found an acquisition. I thanked him, saluted, and turned to go. He called me back:

"By the way," he said, "You'd better get your hair cut. You're not on the stage now."

FIFTEEN

The War in California

June saw me posted abroad. To Canada, I expected. At least, that was the information I was first given; then I was given instructions to take civilian clothing with me. The middle of June found me en route for Iceland. I cannot let Iceland pass without recalling the remark of one of the Q.A.I.N.S. (Queen Alexandra's Imperial Nursing Sisters) who crossed from Glasgow with us. I met her in Reykjavik about two days after we disembarked and asked her what she thought of Iceland.

"Oh, it's all right," she said. "But I just can't go to sleep all day at night."

And I found myself in hearty agreement with her, for I, too, found it most disturbing to wake up in the middle of the night to find the sun streaming in through my windows.

During my two weeks' stay in Iceland I was asked by the officer in control of the Services Radio Station if I would appear on one of his programmes. Of course I said I would. Following the broadcast he invited me back to his mess for a drink. There was but one officer present when we went in, and of course I was introduced. Whereupon the officer to whom I had been introduced burst out with: "I know Martyn Green. That man's an impostor. Place him under immediate arrest. I will get in touch with the Provost." It took me half an hour to convince him that I was who I said I was, and it was not until I discovered that we had a mutual friend in the person of the now late Bishop Salisbury, the Right Reverend Bishop Lunt, then Bishop of Ripon, that he really believed me.

I left Iceland on the day that the United States fleet sailed in. I sailed on board H.M.A.M.C. *Maloja*, a converted P. & O. passenger liner, with eighty R.A.F. Flying Training Cadets who were en route for flying training in the United States. The *Maloja* was the naval escort vessel to a convoy of 140 merchant ships. We were exactly one month at sea, and had, on the whole, a not unpleasant voyage apart from fog and the occasional submarine "flap." I managed to relieve the tedium of the voyage a little by arranging and producing a concert aboard. Naturally we were short of female talent, but I got over the difficulty by shanghaiing the ship's "middy" into some impersonations. Barring the fact that he was nineteen years of age with a good strong growth of beard, he made a very good "woman"—until he opened his mouth. He had a bass voice Chaliapin would have envied. Well, perhaps not so tuneful, but equally deep. The two ship's doctors, a petty officer gunner, two of my R.A.F. cadets, and a leading stoker made a very fine chorus. On the whole, a lively evening was had by all.

We pulled into Halifax about dusk one evening. After dinner I thought I would take a stroll on deck, and got the shock of my life. Lights were blazing away on shore. I stared, amazed. Then I heard the sirens go. I jumped. Then a voice behind me said: "This is Halifax, Canada. They don't have a blackout here—and that siren is only a train."

I should have known, of course, for I'd heard the sound of a

Canadian train before. Two hours later I was ashore enjoying a lighted street once again.

California was my eventual destination. I was posted to one of the six British training schools in the United States as administrative officer, or adjutant—an extremely fortunate posting for me. I would be quite likely to meet a number of old friends, thought I. And I was not far wrong. I also met a number of new friends. The first person I met was Paul England; the next was Reginald Gardiner. For the first few days I began to wonder if I had left England; it was so difficult to meet an American.

My final destination was the Mojave Desert, some eighty-two miles north of Los Angeles. A new flying training school was being built. It was my job to open it and get the wheels running smoothly before the main body arrived. I went out there first with the senior course, a total of fifty cadets just ready to commence on their advanced training with just a sufficient number of instructors to cover their needs. All the instructors were American; the R.A.F. staff consisted of a chief flying instructor, a chief ground instructor (also acting as commanding officer), and an administrative officer—myself, in a supervisory position. No accommodation had been provided for either the instructor or R.A.F. officer staff, so that meant fixing ourselves up with rooms of some sort. I managed to find what they called a duplex available for rent, which I took for the C.O. and myself—but there was no linen provided.

It looked as if we would have to mortgage our pay for the next month or so fitting ourselves out with the necessary bedding, towels, and table linen, until Ronald Colman and his wife, Benita Hume, came to our assistance and gave us everything we needed. I still don't know how they heard of our dire need,

but their offer was most gratefully accepted. I had met Ronald
Colman back in 1929 when in Los Angeles with the D'Oyly
Carte. I remembered the meeting well, and he said he did—but
I have a feeling it was but "mere politeness to a comparative
stranger." Benita I had admired "from the front" many times
in theatres in England but had not met before. That was my
misfortune. I found her just as charming off stage as on.

Maria Montez was a frequent visitor to the airfield, though
perhaps not so frequent as the cadets would have liked. She
was for a time engaged to one of them, a Chilean by the name
of Leitch. Where they met and how they met, I do not know,
but Leitch, with the remainder of his course, was out one day
on a cross-country night training flight. The course planned
was triangular, and really quite simple, with easily recognisa-
ble landmarks requiring little nagivation. It was a "solo" flight
—that is to say, they flew unaccompanied by any instructor.
All aircraft had returned to base within a few minutes of
their E.T.A. (estimated time of arrival) with the exception of
Leitch. He was some time overdue, and some worrying was
going on among the staff and instructors. A telephone call from
about a hundred miles the other side of the Mexican border set
all worries at rest as regards his safety. He explained that he had
lost his way.

A week later a small dance was given in the Cadets' Hall
by the cadets. Leitch arrived with—Maria Montez! From that
moment on every cadet in the place was wondering how *he*
could manage to lose his way on the next cross-country training flight—night or otherwise. Of course, he didn't do it de-
liberately, and Maria wasn't the cause. For one thing, she was
not in Mexico at the time. But it put the idea into the boys'
heads, and they ragged Leitch unmercifully.

I was an occasional visitor to Maria's very lovely house in Beverly Hills and came to know her quite well. She was beautiful—and knew it. She possessed great charm—and never failed to exercise it. It was a great shock to read of her death a short time ago.

These young cadets took Hollywood by storm. They were hailed as young heroes, and we of the R.A.F. Supervisory Staff had a rather difficult job at first to convince them that they weren't—yet. It was our C.O.—Squadron Leader T. G. Whitlock—who finally convinced them. His method of doing so was simple. Final roll call was at 9 P.M. and "lights out"—for all not on night-flying duties—at 9:30 Sunday to Thursday inclusive. An additional hour was allowed on Fridays, and they were allowed to stay up until midnight on Saturdays. One all-night pass from noon Saturday to 9 P.M. Sunday was given every four weeks—provided they could produce evidence as to where they were staying overnight. This was topped off with a lecture in which he told them that they were there to do a job of work learning to fly, and as for being heroes—no man was a hero until he was dead. It had the desired effect, and I think I can say that when the school was eventually closed—as a British training school—they left behind them an enviable reputation. A reputation for good manners, good behaviour, and sportsmanship.

Invitations to parties poured in, of course. The whole of Hollywood seemed to vie with one another in entertaining them. It was part of my job to sort these invitations out, and to see that no cadet got either more than his share or than was good for him. When it was a case of the whole school being invited it was simple, as in the case of the parties given by Miriam Hopkins and Mary Pickford. However, things sorted themselves out, and on the whole they enjoyed themselves as well as doing their job. That they did their job well is proved, I think, by the record of the school: Of the 500 cadets who passed through it, 66 per cent qualified as pilots, 10 per cent being immediately commissioned; among the honours received by past cadets there was one V.C.—Bill Reid—two or three D.S.O.'s, and many D.F.C.'s. A record of which the school, the instructors, the staff, and the cadets themselves may rightly be proud.

The first party to which all were invited was one given by Miriam Hopkins. It was a glorious day in August, and within five minutes of arrival every cadet was in the swimming pool. It would be impossible to name everybody present, but among them Ronald Colman worked like a slave behind the bar serving cooling drinks. Heather Thatcher, looking delightfully cool in a large sunhat, shorts, and sandals, with the inevitable monocle in her eye and a very beautiful diamond wrist watch, stood on the edge of the pool chaffing with the boys in it. What it was that one of the boys said to her I don't know, but she screamed she would "get him for that" and then took one flying leap in—sunhat, shorts, sandals, monocle, diamond watch and all.

The party was topped off with a visit to Grauman's famous Chinese Theater. I don't know how many cars were used to transport everybody there, but a dozen or more mobile police assembled in the driveway of Miriam Hopkins' place and with a continuous shrieking of sirens cleared all traffic to one side while the complete entourage sailed down Sunset Strip and Hollywood Boulevard, ignoring all traffic lights and generally disrupting everything. Quite an experience for the cadets, but, I thought, a little unnecessary and slightly ostentatious.

Another time one of our instructors, Bud Ernst, came to me saying:

"I've got an aunt in Hollywood, and she'd like to give a party one Sunday for the boys. Is that O.K.?"

"I should think so," I said. "Who is she?"

"Mary Pickford," says he.

I had not seen Mary Pickford since 1929, when she and Douglas Fairbanks were frequent visitors to the theatre and gave one or two small parties for Henry Lytton, Bertha Lewis, and a few others of the D'Oyly Carte. I was not averse to meeting her again and told Bud to go ahead with the arrangements. Once more it was a perfect day and the boys had a wonderful time. Two buses were arranged to transport them there and back, and there was practically a 100 per cent turnout.

Ouida Rathbone, niece of Basil Rathbone, also gave a party for some of the cadets. The weather, as usual, was typical California summer, bright sun, and warm. Several of the guests were swimming about in the pool. For some reason or other none of the cadets had brought any swim suits with them, and all were dying to go in. I think it was Heather Thatcher who solved the problem for them. She commandeered all the towels she could raise in the house and a large number of safety pins. That done, she proceeded to fit out those of the boys who so desired in such a fashion that every one of them gave the appearance of being an oversized infant. But the towels served their purpose, and not one of the diapers gave way.

One of my jobs was the meeting of visiting V.I.P.'s who were travelling by ordinary passenger aircraft as opposed to Service aircraft that landed direct on our own airfield. All passenger aircraft came in at Glendale Airport, some sixty or seventy miles from the school. To carry out this duty I had to buy a car, as no service transport was provided and public transport in the shape of the Southern Pacific—the only railroad that passed through Lancaster, our nearest station—was limited to two trains a day. Practically all of these V.I.P.'s (important only by virtue of the fact that they were always senior in rank to myself, usually Group Captains or Wing Commanders) were R.A.F. specialists on tours of inspection, and without exception they were not keen on driving straight out to the airfield immediately on arrival. Our opening conversation usually went something like this:

I would salute, and then:

"Group Captain Snooks, sir?"

"Yes," returning the salute.

"Flight Lieutenant Green of No. 2 B.F.T.S. reporting to meet you, sir."

"Oh, good. How far is the airfield from here?"

"About seventy miles, sir. I have made you a reservation at the Lancaster Inn."

"Seventy miles, eh? What time do you cease flying?"

"Five o'clock, sir. Unless there is any night flying."

"Any tonight?"

"No, sir."

"How far is Hollywood?"

"About seven miles, sir. I have made a tentative reservation for you tonight at the Hotel ——."

"Well, what are we waiting for? Let's get cracking."

"I have my car here, sir."

A fair knowledge of Hollywood was, therefore, pretty necessary to me. It was soon acquired, and I eventually mapped out a sort of itinerary for the would-be revellers and, having once set them on the proper course, was generally able to leave them to follow either this itinerary or their own devices. I personally kept to my own favourite places. One of those was Ella Campbell's—a quiet unobtrusive restaurant on the Sunset Strip owned and run by an Englishwoman of that name. Ella had for some time been the chef at the famous Cock 'n Bull, also on the Sunset Strip, well known for, among other things, its steak and kidney pie. After she left them and opened up for herself, Ella continued to do her own cooking, and her steak and kidney pie lost nothing in the transfer. Most Sunday evenings would find me dining there, and any other evening that duty, in the shape of a V.I.P., might take me there. Unlike the Cock 'n Bull, Ella's place was never overcrowded; just nicely full, all of which was conducive to an enjoyable meal.

I was just finishing a meal one Sunday evening when three men came in and took stools at the bar. I thought I recognised the back of one, so when I had finished I also went to the bar. I was right: it was Jack Barrymore. I was in uniform, Pearl Harbor being a thing of the past and America in the war. Being thus attired I didn't think I would be recognised—and at first I was not. My uniform intrigued Jack at first and he kept glancing at me. Then a flicker of recognition dawned in his eye. He leapt from his stool, rushed over and flung one arm round my shoulder, exclaiming:

"Martyn Green, you old bastard—(a term of affection from Jack)—what in hell's name are you gotten up like a Hollywood actor off the lot for?"

Why I wasn't carried back to my hotel on a stretcher that night I shall never really know. I had to eat another dinner to start with. That finished, I was whisked off to Chasen's, from

Chasen's to the Copa de Ora, to Mike Romanoff's, to the Trop-
ics. Jack *was* carried home. I saw him about twice more after
that before he was taken with his last illness.

Another of my favourite places was the "phony Prince's"
—Mike Romanoff's. I was likely to run into any number of
people I knew. A frequent diner there was Conrad Veidt. For
some reason a number of people saw a great likeness between
me and Conrad. Quite frequently he and I would meet at Mike
Romanoff's, often as not without prearrangement, and being
alone would sup together. One evening, about halfway through
our dinner, a young deb, who had obviously been told that
Conrad Veidt was there, came over to our table with one of
the large menus in her hand. Rather shyly she handed it to me
with the request:

"Could I have your autograph, please?"

I realized she had made a mistake and was on the point of
passing it over to Conrad when I caught his eye, so I smiled at
the girl (I was not in uniform, of course; I was taking a "forty-
eight" and the privilege that went with it of getting into mufti),
took my pen from my pocket, and signed her menu. That done,
I indicated Conrad and murmured, in as near an accent to his
as I could manage, "Veree famous!" and passed the menu to
him. He took it, looked at what I had written, produced his own
pen, signed, and handed it back to the girl with a smile. She
thanked us both very prettily and went back to her table and
party. Should the girl in question ever read this, I hope she will
forgive the deception that she herself created.

I do not want the reader to run away with the idea that my
period of service with the R.A.F. in California was just one
continuous round of Hollywood restaurants, night clubs, and
film stars. Our job on the airfield was pretty strenuous and

entailed many long, weary, and sometimes anxious days and nights. I think I may say that it was only owing to the constant vigilance and care of the R.A.F. supervisory staff that our accident rate was kept below 5 per cent, our major accident rate at approximately 2 per cent, and fatal at .5 per cent. It is regrettable to have to record that from the day the American Air Corps began to take the field over and we began to depart, the accident rate for the field rose sharply, fatal taking the lead. But that was their pigeon; our records remained as before.

Each of the cadets coming to any one of the B.F.T.S.'s had been through an initial training period of approximately eight weeks, and latterly had had at least ten hours' flying. Imagine my surprise when one day a young fellow in mufti walked into my office and handed me a letter that instructed us to take him on the strength of the school, but not on the strength of the R.A.F. He was to commence flying training, forthwith, and with the latest arrived course. He had no initial training—in fact he had no service training of any description; what was more, he had what on paper looked like an unpronounceable name—Ciekenowski.

Further perusal of the letter of instructions revealed that he had been educated in England and spoke the language like a native; that he was a good Rugger player; that he could box; and that he was the son of the Polish Ambassador to the United States. Finally, he was mad keen to get into action. Before he had been with us forty-eight hours he was "the Chicken" to everybody—as much for the fact that he was no bigger than a bantam cock as the suggestion in his name, which we learned was pronounced "Chickenovsky." Starting with a handicap of eight weeks' less instruction than the remainder of his course, he finished up six months later by receiving the Civilian Operator of the Schools plaque for Best Cadet in School. His father happened to be in Los Angeles the day he, with the rest of that course, "passed out" and received his "wings," and was invited to attend the ceremony and present both "wings" and sergeants' stripes—every cadet being automatically promoted to that rank, whether he was to be commissioned or not. Immediately following the "wings" ceremony a sealed envelope was handed to M. Ciekenowski containing the name of the selected Best Cadet. Never have I seen such pride on a father's face as there was on his when he read his son's name out.

Another of our cadets, in this case a regularly enlisted airman, was Robin Sinclair—the son of Sir Arthur Sinclair, the Wartime Minister for Air. Another was Air Marshal Freeman's son. These two boys proved their value to us in no ordinary way. The R.A.F. Supervisory Staff consisted of our Chief Flying Instructor, Squadron Leader Stuart Mills, D.F.C.; Squadron Leader T. G. Whitlock—T. G. for short—the Chief Ground Instructor and Officer Commanding, and myself. When the school was first opened it was situated at what had been the Grand Central Airport. When the new field at Lancaster, Mojave, was approaching completion and able to take the No. 1 course in their advanced training, they were moved over with myself in command. The two subsequent courses—we eventually had four going at the same time—remained behind.

This splitting up of the school necessitated a considerable amount of travelling back and forth on the part of the officer staff, and cars were the only means of transport. These, as I have explained before, we had to buy ourselves (mine cost me $250—more than a month's pay), without any form of financial assistance from the Service. All we were entitled to receive was five cents a mile expenses for all journeys undertaken in the course of duty, and ten dollars a night subsistence money should our duty necessitate staying overnight, as it frequently did.

Application for the payment of these allowances was made every month, with every item enumerated, and was supposed to be paid to us along with our normal pay and allowances cheque at the end of the following month. What with the rents of our quarters, living expenses, original cost of our cars, up-keep, provision of oil and petrol, and several overnight hotel expenses, the financial status of us three officers was pretty grim by the end of the first month.

When at the end of the next month the expected payment of allowances due did not materialize, the outlook assumed an even darker hue. When they still failed to materialize at our next pay day, matters became serious. Letters, telegrams, even a long-distance phone call to R.A.F. Delegation Headquarters in Washington failed to evoke a response. "The matter is re-ceiving attention," "They are expected to be forwarded to all outstations shortly," and similar answers were all the satisfac-tion we could get.

When a further month went by without result our situation became desperate. Duty runs still had to be carried out; petrol and oil had to be bought; rents had to be paid, and food sup-plied—drinks by this time had become but a rapidly fading memory. We held a conference and it was decided that desper-ate situations require desperate action: a "signal" should be des-patched immediately to the senior personnel officer in Wash-ington, Group Captain Trott, who, we felt sure, must be aware of our plight. The secretary was sent for and the following "signal" dictated and sent:

"Sdn/Ldr Whitlock, O.C. 2 BFTS to G/C Trott, Sen. Per-sonnel S.O. Rafdel, Washington. Ref. check rides stop LACs

Sinclair and Freeman on point of elimination stop signal instructions stop PS what about our allowances."

In less than six hours a reply was received. It read:

"G/C Trott, S.P.S.O. Washington to S/L Whitlock, 2
BFTS, Lancaster. Cal. On no account eliminate stop check ride
again stop allowances air mailed repeat mailed noon to day."

We never found out why these allowances had been held up
for so long, nor did we ever discover whether our signal had
been taken seriously or not. Needless to say, we got our allowances the following morning—and neither Sinclair nor Freeman was given another check ride. Their imminent elimination
from flying training had been a pure figment of our imaginations. Both finished high up in their final examinations, passing
with honours and being recommended for commissions.

After Pearl Harbor, the training of the British in the United
States had to be heavily curtailed and eventually almost cease.
Our school was one of the first to be requisitioned by the United
States forces, and we began to close down in June of the following year, but it was not until February of 1943 that we
eventually handed over to the USAAC.

Before sailing for England in the *Queen Elizabeth* I had a
few days' leave in New York, where I renewed acquaintance
with several old friends of the happier pre-war days. Altogether
I had nine days—nine all too few and all too short days. Everybody wanted to give me a party—and I verily believe that most
of them did. At one party given by Marion Ross I had taken
the liberty of inviting the R.A.F. Embarkation Officer. His
reply was that he didn't think he could make it, as he had a
party of V.I.P.'s from Washington arriving and they would
probably keep him hard at it until well on towards midnight.
I said: "Well, come along then." He wasn't too sure, but even

if he did it would only be for a very short while. At five minutes past twelve he arrived with two of the V.I.P.s' staff in tow
—a wing commander and a flight officer of the W.R.A.F. They
departed at 3:30 A.M.

I have to blame Alec Templeton for that. Inevitably he found
his way to the piano. He knew most of the people present, but
he did not know these three. He kept them completely en-
thralled when he began to extemporize in both music and verse,
each verse being based on one of the guests present, describing
them, their work, their looks, their voices, and what he imagined them to be, and generally summing them up. At first
they were inclined to believe that I had given him some prior
information, but I pointed out that as they had practically gate-
crashed the party I obviously could not have had any knowledge of them before their arrival.

But my embarkation orders came all too soon and I was eventually driven down to the dockside, where the *Queen Elizabeth*
was waiting, laden with presents—mostly in shape of bottles.
People seemed to be aware that Scotch was a very rare com-
modity in Great Britain. All these bottles I had had to place
in a sack which, carefully as I might carry it, clanked with
the unmistakable clink of glass on glass. It was in my mind to
preserve it until I reached England, but the dice were loaded
against me. The first person I met going aboard was an air marshal who looked suspiciously at my sack. I explained that it was
a quantity of "medicine" I was taking aboard. He smiled and
said:

"A wise precaution, I understand."

A cryptic remark, I thought. I was soon to learn what he
meant. The *Queen Elizabeth* was, as were all ships by this time,
dry. However, thought I, two bottles should see me through

the trip and still leave me a round half dozen to take ashore.

The very next person I met was my late flight sergeant from California—an N.C.O. who had been sent out to assist on the disciplinary side and to instruct in armament. I couldn't let him drag out the voyage without some sort of sustenance and invited him up to my quarters. When later the air marshal asked me how my medicine was eking out there was only one thing to do—invite him. As I've said in an earlier chapter, I had the best two-berth cabin on the ship, only there were ten of us in it. Fortunately the majority of them had brought something with them, but even so my eight bottles were looking very, very sick when we got to the Clyde. But I must say that it was a great joy to see my flight sergeant clinking glasses with the air marshal and both of them condemning Hitler and his crew to eternal hellfire.

Yes—for close on two years the war in California was pretty good.

I did have one nasty shock when a friend of mine in New York rang me up one day at our airfield to ask me if I were still alive. My C.O. happened to have picked up one of the extension phones, and before I could reply had answered the enquiry with:

"Yes, unfortunately—"

Then I spoke, confirming his unflattering statement and trusting that his face was rapidly turning a deep puce. He continued his statement with:

"Oh, you're there, are you? I was about to say unfortunately you were not in and unable to verify the fact for yourself. Now that you are you can assure your friends yourself."

The enquiry was perfectly genuine, though, and brought about by a radio news commentator—Bide Dudley by name—

by whom I had been interviewed on his programme several times during my visits to New York in the halcyon days of '34, '36, and '39. Apparently he had been rung up by a woman who had read of the death in a flying accident of a cadet at one of the other of the British flying training schools in the United States. What she said I know not, but Bide announced on his programme that "he felt sure lovers of Gilbert and Sullivan in America would be sorry to hear that Martyn Green had been killed in action."

I could only assure my long-distance enquirer, like Mark Twain, that the report was grossly exaggerated. Relieved by my assurance, they rang off and at once rang Bide Dudley's office and informed him of his error. The following evening I had the pleasure of listening to the contradiction of the report of my own death. I assure you, it is quite a pleasure.

SIXTEEN

The Best View of India

*On my return from the United States I took the earliest oppor-*tunity of volunteering for an overseas posting again. I was quietly informed that I probably did not stand an earthly, and it certainly looked that way, for I was posted to South Wales, where I spent six months. Out of the blue one morning my local H.Q. got me on the phone and informed me that I had been posted to India, and that I had better get cracking and hand over to my opposite number at Swansea, as I was to report at Group Headquarters forty-eight hours later. Five days later, after a hurried forty-eight hours' leave, I left London for the North—Blackpool—for kitting, inoculations, vaccination, etc.

I was about five days in Blackpool. Before the end of the next seven weeks I had been vaccinated five more times. Once on the ship before landing; twice in Bombay, and three more times in New Delhi. After that, they gave it up. Not one of the vaccinations "took."

We sailed in convoy, of course; a convoy of seven or eight ships, maybe more. My old friend the *Maloja* was on our starboard side, she having been reconverted from armed merchant cruiser to troopship. I was on the *Strathaird*. Within twenty-four hours I had been elected Entertainments Officer for the ship, rather against my will in the first instance. However, I set to work. We would be at sea for both Christmas and New Year's, and something had to be done about it. I called for volunteers, and I felt, when I saw the response, that 90 per cent of the ship had turned up. I had two staunch helpers, though, and I am pleased to say that on Christmas Day we put on three separate and distinct concerts simultaneously: one in the men's dining hall, one in the warrant officers' lounge, and one in the officers' lounge. That was in the afternoon. In the evening, we switched them round. New Year's Day they were switched again.

We were fortunate in having a number of W.R.N.S. ratings aboard, and female talent was found there. It also enabled us to run dances, for which we were able to form an extremely good dance band. Two accordionists aboard made it possible to send out small "touring" parties to the various mess decks every evening, and a galaxy of talent in the form of some excellent pianists to put on a piano recital every Sunday evening. Time passed very quickly, as far as I was concerned, our five weeks or more seeming little more than one. Barring a few air-attack scares while passing through the Mediterranean, I think a fairly pleasant voyage was had by all—for a troopship, that is.

I did have one unhappy experience. I was the officer in charge of a baggage party going down into the hold of the ship. To get to the baggage hold it was necessary to descend through two hatches. Someone had turned the light off. I knew where the switch was, told the men to wait, and went across to switch on—but someone had left the hatch cover off, and not only that hatch cover but the one immediately below as well. I descended through them both, more rapidly than I had intended.

Believe me, falling a distance of two decks in the pitch dark is not funny. No bones were broken, fortunately, so I picked myself up and mounted the ladder to the top again. My N.C.O. was on the point of following me just as I reached there. He had apparently been saying something to me as I disappeared and, getting no answer, had moved forward in the direction I had first taken. I think he was the more shaken of the two of us when he saw what he had just missed.

Of India itself I prefer to recall as little as possible. It didn't like me, and I didn't like it. I am one of those unfortunate people who suffer from a particularly unpleasant form of prickly heat, and the two summers I spent there were a miniature form of hell to me, and there were few compensations. I had a certain amount of fun in helping to produce and appear in a production of *Charley's Aunt*. It was put into production first by the Combined Services Wireless Experimental Centre, and we gave two performances at the Centre followed by a week at the principal cinema in Connaught Circus, New Delhi. I played the part of Lord Babberly (Babs), or in other words Charley's Aunt herself. A very modern setting was chosen, and the Aunt wore a modern tweed costume in the first act, changing to a very décolleté evening gown in the second. On the whole it was a successful experiment, and a more than reasonable sum was handed over to the fund for the building of an Open-Air Theatre—Troops, for Use Of.

While I was in India I was asked if I could arrange for permission for a production of *The Mikado* to be put on with an "All Services" cast, for the benefit of the three Services only. I wrote the company that costumes could be provided in India, but we—I—would be grateful if they could see their way, not only to grant this permission—if possible royalty-free, as it was for the benefit of the fighting Services—but also to lend a set of the orchestral parts. I would make myself personally responsible for the safety of these, and for the keeping them out of unauthorised hands so that copies could not be made; also, I would arrange that they would be transported out to India and back to England by Service aerial transport. This, in fact, had been arranged. I received no answer to my request.

There is a story about Sir Arthur Sullivan that I think is worth retelling because it repeated itself in India.

During the original run of *Iolanthe* at the old Savoy—then the very new Savoy—Theatre, Sullivan had slipped in to the back of the circle and was leaning on the rail listening to his own overture to the piece conducted by Alfred Cellier. Quite unconsciously he began to hum some of the tunes to himself. A gentleman standing not two yards from him stretched his arm out and tapped Sullivan on the shoulder.

"Excuse me, sir," he said, "but I came in here to listen to Sullivan's music, not yours."

Sullivan, abashed, immediately ceased humming.

I had been working very late one evening at my office in the secretariat and returned to quarters and the mess with only just sufficient time to take a hurried shower, change into some fresh tropical uniform of the approved pattern for wear during dinner, and dash into the mess dining room for the last serving of that meal. There was a musical evening arranged for that evening, given by means of gramophone records and relayed to members of the mess and their friends on the lawn. I couldn't hear what was going on while eating my dinner, nor was I very much interested, as by this time it was more than half over, if not on the point of coming to an end. My meal finished, I could still hear odd strains of music drifting through, and as I wanted a drink decided I might just as well go out onto the lawn my-self—it was very hot inside—and listen to what might still be left of the programme. As I made my way through I passed the officer operating the machine and asked him if there was much left.

"Yes," he told me, "one or two numbers. But you'd better hurry out—I'm just changing the record and it's about to start."

I hurried out, throwing an order for a drink over my shoul-der to one of the near-by bearers, and adding an imperative "Juldi jow" made for the nearest vacant seat, which happened to be at a table already occupied by one air marshal, two group captains, and a wing commander—I was a very humble flight lieutenant. Asking for, and receiving, their permission, I sat down. My drink arrived, strangely enough, two or three sec-onds later—and the next record began. Judge of my surprise when I heard myself singing "Titwillow" from the H.M.V. recordings of the opera made back in 1933 or thereabouts. Un-consciously I, like Sullivan, began to hum the words and tune to myself. I had not completed many bars when the wing com-mander leaned across, tapped me on the knee and said:

"I think we'd rather hear the man who knows how to sing it, not you." Like Sullivan, I shut up—abashed.

As a story against myself it should finish there—but it did not. Without any effort from me the story actually finished—but don't let me anticipate.

The musical evening over, everybody began to drift away, some to their quarters, some to see their friends away or take them home, depending largely on the sex of the guest, and some to the bar, which would not be closing for another hour at least. I was among the last group. Shortly after I reached the bar the president of our Messing Committee came in followed closely by my late table companion—to wit, the wing commander. The P.M.C. greeted me, turned to the wing commander, and said:

"Do you know each other?"

He replied, rather frigidly, I thought, "We sat for a moment at the same table on the lawn, but I can't say we met."

"Oh," said the P.M.C. "this is Flight Lieutenant Martyn Green—Martyn, this is Wing Commander Snooks." (Not his real name, by the way.)

I murmured a polite "How do you do, sir?" and held out my hand.

"How do—" the Wing Commander began; then, "What did you say his name was?"

"Martyn Green," replied the P.M.C.

"Martyn—oh! Christ!"

One of the very first faces I saw on arrival in New Delhi was that of Burgess Meredith. We were in the same camp together for a week or two—a mixed camp accommodating both United States and British officers. Another was Oliver Wakefield. We were in the same mess for some months. Bruce Belfrage, Phillip Charlot (who had been associated with me in the film of *The Mikado* as one of the chief cutters), Peter Donald (of Dundee, and part owner of His Majesty's Theatre there), Glenn Byam-Shaw—all were actively concerned and working with the same directorate as myself, The Directorate of Services Kinematography. My work in connection with that often brought me into contact with Jack Hawkins, who was the principal liaison officer between ENSA and the forces in India.

Had it not been for these folk it would have been unbearable, in spite of the good comradeship I found among all the other of my fellow officers. It has been said by many that the only good view of India is "from the tail end of a ship through the wrong end of a pair of binoculars." I am inclined to agree. I sailed home eventually in the *Durban Castle* in early August, 1945. As we pulled away from the quay I stood at the appropriate end of the ship with my binoculars in my hand obtaining the "best view," with the added attraction of hearing a military band playing the appropriate tune—"There's a troopship just leaving Bombay."

I stood there for some time after the strains of the song had died away and the coast line was beginning to fade in the distance. And then I suddenly realised that the coast line was on our *port* side instead of the starboard. We were going south. Two days later we pulled into Cochin. We lay there for almost another two days while the captain fretted and the troops fumed. The purpose? To embark another fourteen hundred or more troops who had taken train from Bombay four to six hours after we sailed. I was standing on the deck idly watching the embarkation when a woman turned and said:

"Typical, isn't it? I said good-by to my husband just over there," pointing to a spot some five hundred yards away, "a fortnight ago when I left here for Bombay to catch this ship. He can't come aboard and I'm not allowed ashore. I think I'm going to cry."

She did.

On the whole that voyage was not unpleasant. The ship was still dry, but forethought on the part of several of my brother officers and myself overcame that to a certain extent; both the European and Japanese wars were over, and the ship was no longer darkened; and smoking was allowed on deck after dark, all of which helped to relieve the tedium of life aboard a troop-ship.

Shortly after my return I was offered a job to go out to India with Roger Livesey in an ENSA production of *School for Scandal* in the part of Peter Teazle. I was on the point of accepting when I bethought me of prickly heat, mosquitoes, crickets, and the other hundred and one discomforts I had suffered, and I firmly said No. Once was enough.

SEVENTEEN

Back Again

My R.A.F. career came to an end two days after I landed at Liverpool, fairly early in the September of 1945. The organisation for the demobilization of returning overseas troops was perfect. They did not appear to be able to get rid of us fast enough—a fact for which the majority of us were extremely grateful.

Once free of the Service and back again in Civvy Street, I settled down to an extended holiday. There were two reasons for this: one, because I badly needed one, and two, because I had not got a job and there did not seem to be any prospect of one for some time. The theatre was in a bit of a chaotic state, with so many actors and actresses returning from various forms of service. I did a couple or three broadcasts, but it was a month or two before they came around. I attended meetings at the Criterion Theatre for the purpose of discussing the rehabilitation of the ex-service professional. I put into motion an idea for producing a revue or some form of musical entertainment under the auspices of the Sunday Services Society with the idea of getting managers and agents in to see it and the performers taking part. Originally I intended to be in it myself, but somehow or other it gradually slipped out of my and my co-operators' hands and we found ourselves standing on the outside.

In the meantime I had renewed my acquaintance with Sir Malcolm Sargent. Richard Collett had rung me up one day to ask me to go and lunch with him at the Savoy. I did this, and we had a very long and friendly chat about nothing at all. I was wondering why he had invited me to lunch when he asked if I would be willing to appear in one of the Famous Men Birthday Programmes that the B.B.C. were putting out with Sir Malcolm. His Birthday requests had included a wish to conduct some Gilbert and Sullivan again. I said I would, and the result was that I sang the "Nightmare Song" from *Iolanthe*.

That was the beginning of several visits with Collett, all of which got me wondering why. We were very good friends, but not, I felt, so good as to warrant all that unless there was something behind it. He mentioned the United States several times, each time saying how much he would like to go back again—wouldn't I?

Dicky Collett went down with a stroke on New Year's Eve, 1945. He was due to join my wife and me at the Savoy Restaurant. I saw him once during the evening, when he waved, rather vaguely I thought. When the time that he was to join us was long past I made some enquiries, but nobody seemed to know where he was. Later, I heard that he had had a stroke less than a couple of hours after I saw him.

For the next four months I saw nothing of him, but in April of 1946, he rang me up and said if I was free Mr. Carte would like me to lunch with him. I accepted. Over lunch we talked of anything and everything. That was usual. Lunch at an end, we retired to his office. Had I ever thought I would like to return to the company? I supposed I had; I couldn't really say. I had been kept extremely busy since 1939 and had hardly had the time to give it thought. This much I said—but I did not say that I never for one moment expected him to suggest that I should. However, he did suggest it, and two weeks later I signed a contract to open with them in September.

Dicky was there when I came out of Carte's office after signing my contract. He wrung my hand, told me how glad he was, and took me off for a drink to celebrate, saying it was going to be like old times once again. After that I saw him frequently, and we arranged one of our typical week-ends down at his place near Esher. I never went for that week-end, nor did he ever see my re-opening with the company, to which he had looked forward. He complained of a pain after lunch one Sunday, retired to bed, and lapsed rapidly into unconsciousness, from which he never recovered.

When Richard Collett died I lost a good friend, and Rupert D'Oyly Carte a man whom neither he nor his successors will ever be able to replace. A man of great personal charm, a great arbitrator when arbitration was necessary; a man of great tact; a man with authority, who could be firm where firmness was needed; one who never at any time, so far as I knew, bore a grudge or allowed malice to enter into any of his actions; who said what he had to say, whether it was to praise or chastise, and having said it, dropped it—and probably asked you to go and have a drink immediately after. Even his weaknesses had their charm. As King Gama says of King Hildebrand in the last act of *Princess Ida*, "He never could resist a pretty face!" His epitaph could read with truth: "He was fair to all men; all women were fair to him." Not such a bad epitaph, really.

There were many changes in the company when I eventually rejoined it. Sydney Granville had retired during the war, and his parts had been taken over by Richard Walker. J. M. Gordon was dead—he died in 1941, practically in harness, as he would have wished. Freddie Hobbs had gone, too. So had Leonard Rooke, who for years had been the Advance Publicity and Press Relations Manager to the company and who had taken over Business Management on Fred Hobbs's death. Leonard's post of Advance Publicity and Press Relations Manager is one that has never been filled since. That may account for the great lack of publicity the company has suffered in the last few years, though even he was limited as to the extent to which he could go. When he died—in 1945, I believe it was—the business management was taken over by Bob Jones, who had recently been filling the position of Assistant Stage Manager under Harry Arnold after some twenty-odd years in the chorus.

Harry Arnold had been combining the positions of stage director and stage manager until Carte brought in Anna Bethel, in the early part of 1947. Harry left practically at a moment's notice. I don't think he could see his way to working under Anna. Frankly, I didn't blame him.

The 1946–47 tour is one I shall not easily forget, if only for the discomforts it produced during the extreme winter, the fuel crisis being responsible for most of the discomfort. Few, if any, of the theatres we visited were heated, and we seemed to spend the worst of the winter in the coldest parts of the country. Sunday travelling was a torture—I had no car at the time, and so had perforce to travel by train in unheated coaches. Yet people braved the snow, the storms, and the inevitable iciness of the theatre to come and watch the shows. I do not exaggerate when I say that it was no unusual thing to see patrons in the front rows wearing overcoats and gloves, with rugs over their knees and in some cases, I discovered, hot-water bottles at their feet.

They had the advantage over us on the stage. I well remember one performance of *Patience* when I, in the velvet costume of Bunthorne, found it extremely difficult to remain seated on the stump during my first entrance scene. I was so cold and shivering so hard that I shivered myself off. And if I was cold in my velvet suit, Heaven knows what the girls in their diaphanous Greek frocks felt like. I know what some of them looked like, for several of them had blue gowns, and it was difficult to know where the frock ended and they began.

But we lived through it, and when spring at last arrived, which it did when we were in Bristol, we appreciated it all the more. The one thing I missed most was my golf. This is the only form of exercise in which I now indulge; ever since my fall through the open hatches on the *Strathaird* on my way to India, a slipped disc has ruled out my other pastime of riding.

The Sadler's Wells summer season of 1947 saw the reproduction of *H.M.S. Pinafore*—one of the operas that had been almost totally lost during the London Blitz of '40–'41, when an oil bomb fell directly on the company's stores. This was to be Leslie Rands' swan song; Charles Dorning was to succeed him. Four performances were given on the last three days of that season, in which Leslie played the part of Captain Corcoran. After the last performance he retired from the company.

Anna Bethel, or Nan, as she was more familiarly known, was concerned with this reproduction, as she was later with the reproduction of *Ruddigore*—another of the blitzed operas. Nan also accompanied us to America, thus creating a precedent that had been denied J. M. Gordon. I liked Nan, having known her for years as Mrs. Sydney Granville, and worked with her in

Ruddigore when she played the part of Dame Hannah at several performances following the death of Bertha Lewis. But as stage director she could be, and was, very naughty at times.

Early December of 1947 saw us in the throes of preparations for the forthcoming visit to the United States—the first since 1939. We sailed on the *Queen Mary* on 19th December, the whole company travelling cabin. Rupert Carte had given a tea party to which the whole company were invited immediately prior to catching the boat train at Waterloo. It was at this party that he informed us that he would be coming over to the United States—in fact, he would be sailing in the same ship. It was rather a pity he did that, for it caused a great deal of comment, particularly among the number of American friends who came to meet the company, for Carte was travelling first class. Once again from a press and publicity angle it did not do him any good, for, though no one remarked on it, there were very few who remarked on the company's arrival at all, and none at any great length.

For years it has been the policy of the D'Oyly Carte Opera Company to frown upon anything other than the most dignified and austere of publicity, and to a large extent quite rightly. But they also frowned upon the presentation of Gilbert and Sullivan in any form or medium other than that of the stage proper, in spite of the fact that three times during the 1951 Festival Season at the Savoy, and several times before the war, excerpts were broadcast from the stage during an actual performance; a couple of abridged versions were put out as studio broadcasts; a film of *The Mikado* was made; and two six-week series at an interval of twelve months on the lives of Gilbert and Sullivan, with excerpts from the works of each, separately and in collaboration, were put out by the B.B.C.

The strange thing is that after every one of these presentations by other mediums the business rose, particularly after the "Lives" series, when on several occasions the police had to be called to control the crowds at the box offices of theatres at which we were due to appear.

Sullivan himself was certainly not unaware of the value of that sort of publicity when, at the time the original production of *H.M.S. Pinafore* looked like a failure, he included an arrangement of the opera's music in a Promenade Concert at the Queen's Hall. The immediate result was a rush for the box office, and a near failure was saved and became a success. During the D'Oyly Carte's last visit to the United States, I was amazed when told by a gentleman intimately concerned with television in America that he had approached the general manager with an offer to give some *free* pre-arrival publicity on television in the form of some short excerpts, previously filmed during a performance, I imagine, and one or two interviews with some of the principals, only to be told, "This is the D'Oyly Carte Opera Company. We don't need that sort of publicity."

I don't know whether it *would* have done us any good or not. It certainly could not have done us any harm, of that I am sure —and the business we did was *not* good during the first half of the tour—not until we reached Chicago. As was pointed out to me by many people, the name D'Oyly Carte did not mean a thing to the large majority of people in the towns and cities which we had not visited before, or not for some ten to thirteen years. It was just another Gilbert and Sullivan company, of which there had been so many and not too good. I cannot help feeling convinced that "that sort of publicity" is most definitely needed—and plenty of it.

We arrived on the morning of the 24th, and by 11 A.M. my wife and I were settling down in what has now become known as "our New York home." A small place—as apartment hotels in New York go—but offering us a welcome hard to duplicate anywhere else. The porter at the door wringing our hands and giving us a "welcome home" before we had time to get out of the taxi. The receptionists; the manager, Mr. D'Arcy; the proprietor, Fritz Christados, leading us to our old apartment and welcoming us with vases of flowers and a bottle of Scotch. But it's not a case of proprietor or manager and hotel guest. It is old friends meeting once again. Yes, for both my wife and myself, Park Chambers is certainly home.

Our traditional lunch at Sardi's followed, where once again an outstanding welcome awaited us. We learned that Vincent Sardi had more or less retired and handed the running of the place over to his son—another Vincent, both in name and ability. In the evening my wife thought she would like to take a walk as far as Broadway and Times Square. We turned into Sixth Avenue—or the Avenue of the Americas, to give it its official title since the Elevated was removed—and had not gone very far when we passed a drugstore. One of its windows was full of soap. Soap of all kinds, bath, toilet, washing powders, and flakes. My wife took one look and then made to dive into the place, saying:

"Soap! I must get some before it all goes."

It took me the best part of ten minutes to convince her that we were in New York, where soap rationing was unknown, and that it would all still be there tomorrow and the next day and the day after that. But it took us both quite a long while to get used to the superabundance of everything, and we found ourselves quite likely to buy something we didn't really want at the moment because we were afraid it might not be there the next time we passed the shop.

We finished up that walk by having some supper at Sardi's. (George) Melville Cooper was in there having a quiet meal by himself, and we eventually joined him for a drink. The evening ended by his inviting us to a "small party" he and his wife were giving in their apartment on Christmas night, which we accepted with alacrity. Most of our friends were out of town for Christmas and we had rather made our minds up to a Christmas *à deux;* not that we minded that—in fact in the main it was *à deux,* as the party was not due to start until somewhere around ten or eleven at night. We ourselves arrived about 11:30. I am still trying to make up my mind as to whether George was alluding to the size of his apartment, or whether his idea of a small party meant approximately fifty people. Whichever it was, he was right in the word he selected, for never have I seen so many people gathered together at the same time in so small a space. We left the party about 2 A.M. in company with another guest who very kindly drove us back to our apartment. It was a glorious night; cold, but bright with the brightness of a fairly hard frost, and I believe I was able to see stars shining through the glitter of Broadway's myriads of neon and electric skysigns. On the whole, a pleasant Christmas Day.

I awoke the following morning—or to be more accurate, later the same morning—leapt out of my bed with the agility of a one-legged centenarian, and glanced out of the window. The view that met my eye was as if someone had taken an immense white sheet and spread it all over New York. It was snowing hard. How long it had been snowing I do not know, but there was something like ten to twelve inches of snow. Cars parked along each side of the street were nothing but vague

outlines; the majority had to stay there until it became possible
to dig them out, and in some cases that meant weeks. By the
time the snow ceased I believe a matter of nearly twenty-six
inches had fallen.

Fortunately the theatres and hotels are warmed—often to
an uncomfortable degree so far as the Englishman is concerned
—so we did not suffer from cold as we did during the previous
winter in England. Regarding the extremes to which they
would go in the matter of overheating, Wendy Hillier told me
that she invariably had a battle royal about it, often having to
go so far as to threaten she would not go on for the second act
unless the heat was turned off. I tried it myself, once, but it
didn't work. All I got was: "This is a big theatre (the New
Century) and if we turn the heat off the auditorium gets cold
very quickly and then we get complaints from the audience,
and they don't come in again."

We opened this season with *The Mikado*—always a good
choice, I think—to a practically full house, in spite of the pre-
vailing weather conditions and the resultant bad traffic conditions. It is interesting to note that although I had appeared in
the role of Ko-Ko many times before the war I received, after
the latest opening, several letters objecting to my use of the
word "nigger" in my first song ("There's the nigger serenader,
and the others of his race"). Darrell Fancourt, I believe, was
also taken to task for his use of the same word in a later song
("The lady who dyes a chemical yellow . . . Or pinches her
figure, Is blacked like a nigger"). Mr. Carte, apparently, received some similar objections, also.

Carte came in to see me and asked me to think out some word
to take its place, which I did, and introduced very shortly after.
The allusion in the first place was not, I am sure, intended to be

interpreted as being an allusion to any race, but to the old-time ministrel shows—the nigger minstrels—and I based my selection of the word I would use on that, my selected word being "minstrel." It scanned, and what was more, to my mind kept the same meaning while avoiding the giving of any offence. Carte said nothing at the time.

As regards Fancourt's use of the word, that was a little more difficult, so Carte left it as it was until he could find something to replace it. To do this he co-opted a well-known poet, playwright, and lyricist—Sir Alan P. Herbert, who produced several lines for Carte to make a selection from. I will never know what prompted him to select the line he did, for to my mind it does not make sense. It now reads: ". . . or pinches her figure, Is painted with vigour, *And* permanent walnut juice." I feel I want to ask what is the colour of "vigour"? I have a great admiration for the work of Alan Herbert—but not of that particular piece. In fairness to him, I must add that he himself does not think a great deal of it. His own pet version Carte would not even consider.

I could not remember what this was when I wanted to quote it, although A.P.H. had told me in the foyer of the Savoy Grill, and I thought I had committed it to memory. It also dawned on me that I had better get his permission to quote it before actually doing so. I called him on the phone—finding it far too difficult to set my wishes down on paper—and to my delight received his permission, provided he could remember it himself. However, he thought that copies would be hanging about somewhere and would let me have one as soon as he found it. By the following morning's post I received a copy with *four* alternatives, including the one now in use.

The selections offered to Mr. Carte I reprint herewith:

(1) The lady who dyes a chemical yellow
     Or stains her grey hair puce,
          Or pinches her figure
          Is painted with vigour
     And permanent walnut juice.

(2) The lady who dyes a chemical yellow
     Or stains her grey hair green
          Is taken to Dover
          And painted all over
     A horrible ultramarine.

(3) The lady who dyes a chemical yellow
     Or stains her grey hair puce
          Is made to wear feathers
          In all the worst weathers
     And legibly labelled "Goose."

(4) The lady who dyes a chemical yellow
     Or stains her grey hair blue
          Wears nothing but feathers
          In all the worst weathers
     And lives in a draughty Zoo.
                    Or
          Is made to wear feathers
          In all the worst weathers
     And kept in a draughty Zoo.

The second of these was Alan's own favourite.

As regards myself, I received a letter from Carte not very long after his return to England telling me that he wished me to use the words "banjo serenader." I wrote telling him that I was already using "minstrel" and couldn't help feeling it was more in keeping with the original intention, to which he replied that he still wished me to use "banjo"—and that word was being printed in all the new editions of the libretto.

I used and continued to use "banjo."

From a weather point of view neither New York nor Boston was kindly disposed to us on that trip. The snow remained until practically the end of our stay in New York, and of the twenty-eight days we spent in Boston twenty-one of them sent us rain, thus putting a most effective stop to any form of outdoor exercise. I managed to get one game of golf, and one only, during the whole of that visit. Not that I did without exercise of any sort. Twice a week at least I would play squash in New York University's very excellent courts, my partners being either Richard Walker or Leo Genn, neither of whom I could ever beat.

I gave several interviews over the air on one or the other of the broadcasting systems. Priscilla Fortescue, who has a "Woman's Hour" spot on the National Broadcasting Company's WEEI Station, Boston, rang me at my hotel one day. My wife answered the phone, and Priscilla told me a couple of years later that her first reaction was "Huh! These snooty limeys!" My wife is not fond of speaking on the phone, and is inclined to speak in monosyllables. I, too, find speaking over the phone something of a trial and become rather stilted in my conversation. That gave Priscilla the impression that we were a little snooty. However, she persevered, and eventually extracted a promise that I would give her an interview. When we eventually met, just before the broadcast, I found her an extremely charming person. I asked her:

"What about a script?"

"Oh, we don't want a script," she replied. "I've got a few questions written down that I want to ask you, and you just give me the answers."

I was both a little bit frightened at the idea, and a little bit relieved. I have always felt that a prewritten interview sounds, on the air, just what it is—prepared—and in consequence becomes rather stilted. Apparently this interview was something of a success, for the next time I was in Boston I did three interviews with her. I also recorded one for her in New York when we reached there after our road tour in '51. Later she came to England for the Festival, when once again I recorded an interview. She even managed to get my wife to do one as well.

This visit of 1947–48 at last came to an end, and I returned to New York for a few days before sailing on the *Mauretania*.

E I G H T E E N

The Beginning of the End

The summer of 1948 saw us once more at Sadler's Wells. At the end of the season we went on tour, and it was then that the great blow fell—the death of Rupert D'Oyly Carte. He had been a very sick man during the earlier part of 1947, and had not, in fact, been expected to recover. His daughter, who was not in town, had been sent for, and everybody was prepared to hear the worst. The day after he had been given up he was sitting up in bed dictating letters. Shortly afterwards he was up and had resumed practically normal activities. Later, as I have related, he came over to New York, where he remained for several weeks. Shortly before we ended our Sadler's Wells engagement in 1948 he went for an extended holiday to the south of France, and, I am told, was more of his old self than he had been since the death of his son. The next we heard was just after we started out on the new tour. He had been brought home on a stretcher and died shortly after reaching England.

This was a great shock to the company, not so much from a sense of personal loss—he was far too impersonal in his relations with the members of the company for that—but from a feeling of insecurity. His daughter Bridget, his only remaining

232

issue, had never, apparently, shown anything more than a passing interest in the work of the company. I may be misjudging her, and that is why I say "apparently." She had never been active in the affairs of the company, and naturally we all wondered what was going to happen. She assumed control, however, and things appeared to continue along their normal lines. Then, apparently in accordance with the wishes of her father, the word "Limited" appeared at the end of the company's name, and three more directors were appointed. She herself retained the active control.

Of these other three directors one is the son of a well-known, in fact famous, English actor, and this fact was the cause of a particularly amusing piece of repartee. The then stage director —not Anna Bethel, but the one who followed—was giving some instructions to Richard Watson regarding some stage business with which he disagreed.

"However," he said, "you are the stage director and I suppose I must do as you say."

"These are not my orders," she told him. "I am merely passing on instructions."

"But they're ridiculous," said Richard. "Whose orders are they—Bridget's?"

"No—they are Mr. So-and-so's."

"But what does he know of the stage?"

"What does he know? His father was a famous actor!"

"Oh! Well, my father was a famous surgeon—would you like me to take your appendix out?"

The first major job that Bridget D'Oyly Carte carried out was the reproduction of *Ruddigore* at Newcastle-on Tyne in October of '48. Peter Goffin was again responsible for the décor. There was little change in the first act from the scene as it used to be before the war. A tree had been removed—a set piece—from the near centre of the stage and painted on one of the flats, thus releasing a great deal more stage room; this was definitely a wise move. The second act was almost as violent a departure as *The Yeomen of the Guard* had been. The sombre, ancient, and rather dilapidated appearance of the old Baronial Hall completely disappeared and a much brighter scene took its place, with very new and rather modernistic banners hanging about instead of the torn, faded, and dusty-looking ones of the previous set. But the costuming was the most violent change of all. The Chorus of Bucks and Blades, previously a glittering array of military uniforms of the period approximating to Nelson's time, gave way to the coloured top hats, tail coats, fancy waistcoats, and canes of the dandy man-about-town, presumably of the same period. A brilliant emerald-green motif took the place of the sombre dark grey of Sir Despard's first and Robin Oakapple's second act. An auburn wig replaced the black bow-tied wig that went with the costume. In Robin's first-act redesigned costume I never felt comfortable. The straw hat and coat retained some of the old design, but the corduroy breeches of the young farmer gave way to a skin-tight pair of pale olive-green made of a light pinhead material; the rough brown homespun stockings to a pair of brilliant pillar-box red cotton. Mad Margaret's wild-looking frock and tow-coloured wig with bits of hay sticking in it—as if she had been sleeping under the nearest haystack—was swept aside in favour of a somewhat sickly-looking pale canary-yellow frock that had a touch of the crinoline about it; the wig became ginger. The costumes of the gallery of ghostly ancestors were about the only ones that did not undergo change.

Ruddigore had never been one of the prime favourites with

the public, and would seldom stand more than two performances per visit. On its reproduction, however, it seemed to take
on a new lease of life, and several times I have heard remarks to
the effect that it was one of the best things the company did.
So perhaps Peter Goffin was right with his sweeping changes.
Nevertheless, I had more than one argument with him over the
matter of my costume. I don't know how it was, but we could
never meet to talk about costumes without finishing up with a
heated argument. We dined together a couple of weeks after
the Festival Season of '51 came to an end and discussed this subject, among others, and eventually came to the conclusion that
it may well have been because we were never left to talk about
costumes by ourselves; somebody would be sure to join in with
the talk—the Wardrobe, the Stage Director, the General Manager, Miss Carte.

Once, and once only, were we left alone long enough to
reach an amicable conclusion. There was an addition to my
second-act costume that I wanted. I told Peter what it was and
why I required it. To my intense surprise he said, "I don't see
why not"—but only just in time. We were joined by the inevitable Wardrobe—or whichever one of the many it may
have been—and within five minutes we were fighting again.
We decided, over that dinner, that in the future the chances
were we would be able to fight on a more friendly footing.

I shall never understand why the powers that be failed to
take *Ruddigore* to the United States on the last visit. It was constantly asked for.

Ruddigore was the last major job that Anna Bethel did as
stage director. Not many months after its reproduction she
left the company. Later on—about twelve months later—she
went out to Australia with the Tait and Williamson Gilbert

and Sullivan Company to produce the operas for them. Quite a few of the late members of the company went with her— John Dean, Richard Walker and his wife, Helen Roberts; Leslie Rands and Marjorie Eyre were tempted out of retirement. Evelyn Gardiner was already there, having married and gone out to Australia on the outbreak of war. Richard Walker and Helen Roberts have since left that company and are now making a concert tour of the United States, where they hope to make their home.

The next stage director was another woman: Eleanor Evans —in private life, Mrs. Darrell Fancourt. I had heard there was some possibility of this happening and, at an interview, told Miss Carte that I thought she was making a great psychological error. During Anna Bethel's regime there had been growing signs of discontent and suggestions of favouritism being shown to some of the members of the chorus in respect to passing over existing understudies, selections for small parts, and so on. Also, there were criticisms of her methods or lack of methods of production. I am making no statement myself in respect of these criticisms one way or another; I merely state that they were very much in evidence.

To my mind the appointment of another woman was an error. But to appoint not only a woman who had for fifteen years worked in the chorus alongside several who were now principals, but the wife of one of the main principals, seemed to me to be a psychological error of the first magnitude. I felt that no matter how she behaved, unless she cut herself off from all contact with the company other than at rehearsals or when actually engaged in carrying out her job—and this would have to apply to her husband as well—she would, rightly or wrongly, be accused of that very same favouritism.

My views made no impression on Miss Carte, but time was to prove that I was right. Discontent grew, changes were constantly taking place, and criticism became rampant. Nor did it stop at the methods of production; it went so far as to suggest a complete lack of knowledge, evidenced, so it was said, by constant self-contradiction. There were other accusations levelled against her, of a more serious nature. Again, I only quote from the various whispers that reached my ears. I make no observations either way, other than to repeat that the fault lay in engaging another woman to follow one who had suffered in much the same way. It was bound to turn out the way it has.

If I have any criticisms to make they are of the methods of production as laid down by those in control. It is apparently assumed in the first place that the performers are little more than automatons and are completely devoid of brains or the ability to think for themselves. Production is done to a plan that takes no consideration of the individual, his personality or his histrionic ability—a stereotyped plan that results in a clockwork performance devoid of spontaneity.

Gilbert and Sullivan should sparkle, scintillate from the first note of the overture to the last note of the finale. Sir Malcolm Sargent was frequently criticised by many of the patrons of the theatre, and listeners on the air, and by members of the company (among whom I was to be numbered) for many of his tempos—but there is no doubt that he lifted those performances which he conducted out of the rut of the commonplace; he gave the music a sparkle, and by his own virile personality created an enthusiasm among those on the stage, particularly the chorus, that soon evidenced itself in giving an impression of spontaneity that quickly infected the audience. And yet, in

238 · *Here's a How-de-do*

spite of the virility of his conducting, I do not think he imposed himself on the audience. That is to say, at all times, other than during the overture, the stage was the centre of attraction. His conducting was never at any time heavy-handed. I myself described him as conducting on the "up" beat, and not on the "down." Unfortunately, he only conducted half a dozen performances, each one different, and the company were not given the opportunity of settling down or of fully absorbing and appreciating his methods and interpretations.

Gilbert and Sullivan has not been a life's work with Malcolm. His affection for the works is undoubted, but his study of them is incidental only to his study of music generally. I am convinced that if the powers that be would engage a producer (a director, as they are called in the United States) whose study of Gilbert's works was incidental only to study of the stage, stagecraft, and production in general, and who could approach the operas with an entirely fresh mind, they would assure themselves of performances that would stand the test of any criticism the most cynical of critics might wish to level against them. And it would not be necessary to depart from the framework as built by Gilbert himself, or from the tradition of the operas.

Gilbert himself was twenty years ahead of his time when he produced these operas originally—these comic operas, I should say. Personally, I disagree with the word "opera" in connection with G. & S.—it is misleading. "Comic opera" is better, but I would prefer to see them alluded to as musical plays—musical comedies, musical topsy-turvey-ras, if you like—but opera, no. I am sure that there are many people who are kept away from them by that one word alone. But is it not within the bounds of reason to believe that if Gilbert were alive today he would still be twenty years ahead of his time, and so, while realizing the value of his works even as they are presented today, promptly set about reproducing them more in accordance with the modern stage, while retaining their Victorian charm?

The "new" production of *The Yeomen of the Guard* was an effort in the right direction, going, perhaps a little too far—but it stopped short at the décor, or very nearly so. Perhaps when the rights finally expire and the operas enter the public domain some enterprising producer will present them as they should be. Many will probably attempt to do so, and many will be the failures. Attempts may be made, as they were in the United States, to "hot them up," as witness the two coloured productions in New York just prior to the war—*The Swing Mikado* and *The Hot Mikado*. Let us hope that something may be done to prevent such a thing happening in England.

And yet there is a set of unconventional recordings of several numbers from the Gilbert and Sullivan operas that I very much want to own. I suppose it is really my own fault that I don't already own them, as they were, and probably still are, available in the United States. They are not available in Great Britain. The records I speak of are made by Danny Kaye, and I'm told do not adhere quite as strictly as they should to the script —that is, Gilbert's original script. I've not heard them—yet— but those who have tell me they are extremely funny. It may be a form of sacrilege on my part to want them, but I do.

I first met Danny Kaye in Sardi's in 1951 during our all too short season at the St. James Theatre, New York. I told him that I wanted a set of his records—I had made one or two more or less feeble efforts to obtain them, but as each of the two shops I went into for them had sold out and was waiting for a further stock to arrive I didn't press on with it. Danny's reply was typical:

"*You* want a set. Why, you're the one person I would hate to have a set."

"But I'm told they are extremely good." I said. "And very funny."

"Yes," said Danny, "maybe—but they're not Gilbert and Sullivan. You know, I like Gilbert and Sullivan; I love singing it. I always wanted to make some records of some of them. Then I start, and I start in all good faith to sing it properly and then something goes haywire inside me; I go haywire—and the words go haywire."

My last visit to the United States with the D'Oyly Carte Opera Company was in 1950–51. That tour cannot be counted among our most successful. I think several mistakes were made, the first being that the company was sent on tour without the backing and build-up that a season in New York would undoubtedly have given it. It was almost like going into the United States through the back door—with little, if any, arrival publicity. Our first date was New Haven, where we played four performances only, the extent of our stay being three days. That was followed by three weeks at Boston, where we played at the Boston Opera House, which seats three thousand people. Only once did we fill the theatre—that was on our last Saturday night. Taking things by and large, I suppose we did extremely well, as I imagine we played, on an average, to between 1,200 and 1,800 people a night.

Nevertheless, I had a very enjoyable three weeks there, renewing old acquaintances. Among those I saw was Priscilla Fortescue, with whom I did two or three broadcast interviews, and whom I learned to like more and more with each meeting. The fact that the roles I play are mostly old men, and that it is pretty well known that I first joined the D'Oyly Carte Company in 1922, led to Priscilla having an amusing short conversation with an assistant in a music shop where she was purchasing one of the new long-playing albums of one of the recently re-recorded operas. While he was wrapping her purchase they began to talk of the current visit of the company. My name cropped up, and the assistant said:

"It's sad to think that this is probably the last time we shall see him, isn't it?"

"Whatever makes you say that?" queried Priscilla. "I don't know that he's leaving."

"Oh, but he'll probably have to," replied the assistant. "After all, he can't be expected to go on much longer. Why, he must be well over eighty."

Priscilla's answer to that was to burst out laughing and, on recovering her composure, inform the gentleman that he was some thirty-odd years out. Of this she was pretty certain, as I had been supping with her and her husband only the previous night. On learning this the assistant was so impressed that he almost reached the point of making her a present of the records.

We paid our first visit to Springfield and Providence—giving each three days. I was rather sorry that our stay in Providence was not of much longer duration. My wife and I discovered—not that it took a lot of discovering—an all-night diner. It stood directly across the street from the main entrance to our hotel. It used to be driven up sometime in the evening, while I was at the theatre, and connect up with the city's lighting and power, for which points had been provided. Whether they had been specially provided or not, I cannot say, but it was the means whereby the owners were able to light the interior and obtain heat for cooking. It was about the size of a fairly large motor coach, and with a counter running down the centre for practically its full length, leaving just sufficient room for a cash register, the operator, and a sort of service hatch for serving customers who did not wish to enter, or who could not as it was fully occupied inside. On one side of the counter were a number of stools, fixed to the floor—it could seat about a dozen—and on the other, hot plates, grills, food safes, etc., and two assistants.

We "discovered" the place simply because, after a tiring day, having travelled from Springfield and arrived somewhere about three in the afternoon, arranged everything in my dressing room for the evening performance, and then played Ko-Ko to a not too full or enthusiastic house, I did not feel like indulging in anything approaching a big meal. What I mostly required was a large drink, which we had in the hotel's somewhat ornate bar. It was while having this drink that my wife suggested going over to this diner. After making enquiries of the porter as to the quality of the food, we went across, perched ourselves on a couple of stools, and ordered hamburgers and coffee. We had three apiece. We were only in Providence for two more nights, but both nights found us sitting on these stools eating hamburgers or hot dogs, and drinking coffee—and very good it all was. After reaching Baltimore, our next stop, we looked for a similar place, but found nothing to compare.

A pretty extensive tour had been booked for us that should have taken us through St. Louis and Cincinnati, with a month in Chicago and two weeks in Toronto. Business, however, had been so bad that at one time, shortly after reaching Philadelphia, where we were booked for four weeks—immediately prior to Christmas—the office contemplated abandoning the tour. Our four weeks in Philadelphia was cut to three, and then it was extended again to the original four. Rumours were rife to the effect that we would be sailing for England either before or directly after Christmas.

Later I learned that this actually was contemplated but the Shuberts refused, or at least brought sufficient persuasive powers to bear to alter that decision. But St. Louis and Cincinnati were both cancelled; the Chicago date was brought forward and cut from four to two weeks, and the Toronto date brought forward by some four weeks and cut from two to one. As soon as I heard this I knew a mistake had been made and told our business manager that instead of cutting the dates short they should have left two weeks following the four at Chicago free so that should the demand arise, as I was certain it would, they could "extend the season by popular demand." And similarly at Toronto. That my estimate of the business we could do in both places was correct was proved by the packed houses and the constant demand both at the box office and in the press for an extention.

The company travelled up to Toronto, which followed on Chicago, through the Sunday, leaving at some ungodly hour in the morning. I freely admit that the prospect of arising at the unearthly hour of 6 to 6:30 A.M. did not present a glowing picture, and I booked accommodation on the night train leaving at 7:30, I think it was, and arriving at Toronto 8:30 the following morning.

The Consul General, Mr. Barclay Gage, hearing of this, decided to give me a small farewell party on the Sunday noon— just cocktails, after which we were to lunch with him before returning to the club at which we had been staying to complete our packing and make for the station. Cocktails were from twelve noon to two o'clock—at least that was what the invitation said. As far as I remember, the last guest left somewhere around four and we sat down to lunch in the Pump Room of the Ambassador Hotel at four-thirty. It was not that liquor flowed in excess. It seemed to me that everyone there was rather reluctant to say a final farewell to the last remnant of the D'Oyly Carte Opera Company. And both my wife and I were finding it a little sad to say good-by to many old friends, one of whom was John Barclay, who had played the title role in the film version of *The Mikado*.

We eventually got back to our club, the Union Club of Chicago, with only just sufficient time to throw the remainder of our things into a couple of suitcases and grab a taxi.

On the way to the station the driver suddenly shot over his shoulder:

"You've had a pretty good visit in Chicago, ain't ya, Mr. Green?"

I agreed that we had. He had obviously read the labels on my baggage.

"I bin in to see every one of 'em," he informed me. "The wife and I love 'em."

He paused a minute. "I don't know why you're pulling out. You could've stayed another two months!"

During our week in Toronto we all received a very nasty shock in so far as we all got a demand for income tax. There was no argument about it, we had to pay it, otherwise they would just deduct it. As none of us were receiving full salary at any time during our American engagement, the British Treasury ruling that 25 per cent must be sent back to England —to prevent us spending it, ensuring their getting the dollars— this sudden extra drain on our resources was in many cases causing some hardship and not a little worry regarding the paying of hotel bills, etc., at the end of the week. Representations were made to high authority in Ottawa, but nothing could be done. To make it worse, because we were actors, we had to pay the full rate without any allowances of any description.

We made the journey from Toronto to New York by day. It was good to get back to New York and renew old friendships. But it was a crushing blow to find—after a smashing opening on the Monday at the St. James Theatre, with rave notices in every paper the following morning—a notice pinned up on the board on the Tuesday evening announcing that the season would close just four weeks later. Pressure was brought to bear from all sorts of people and places; the press practically ran a campaign to get the season extended, but to no avail. A bad attack of cold feet just before Christmas had caused the office to hurriedly book dates in England, and having booked them it seems they could not get out of them. Which is understandable. We actually sailed home a full four weeks before we had originally intended.

It is an extremely difficult thing to get a quart into a pint pot, and that is more or less what that visit turned out to be. A problem of trying to fit six months' social obligations into four weeks.

Margaret Truman was a frequent visitor to the theatre during this visit, and we would invariably see her in Sardi's having a light meal after the show. I first met her in Boston when she asked if she might come backstage to see me following a performance of *Iolanthe*. I had wondered on arriving at the theatre before the performance what the extra crowd, and the numbers of police, both mobile and foot, were doing round the main entrance. I found her a very charming and unassuming person but suffering, in Boston, from the constant and close attentions of her Secret Service escort—at least, that is what I assumed him to be. Later, in New York, she was free of these attentions, or at any rate, they were not in evidence. Her father is also a great lover of G. & S., as is her mother, but owing to pressure of State business had found it utterly impossible to take sufficient time off to make the trip either to Baltimore, when we were there before Christmas, or to New York. However, Margaret explained that it was his birthday quite shortly and she was arranging that he should not be entirely robbed of the opportunity of seeing one at least of the operas and had booked the film of *The Mikado* for a private showing at The White House for that occasion.

She expressed regret that the company had not included Washington in our itinerary. Several other people, including Lady Franks, the wife of the British Ambassador, expressed similar regrets—tinged with a little surprise. I myself was very sorry we had not done so, but, as I explained to many people, the theatre to which we had been accustomed was permanently closed; and as that theatre was the only one in Washington it left us no choice but to miss out the capital. To *my* surprise I learned that there was a theatre there now, a new one having recently been opened. Exactly when, I cannot say, so it is possible that it came too late for a booking to be made. One of the party at the table with Margaret suggested that a "command performance" might be arranged, but even if that could have been arranged it was far too late then.

I cannot say that our business at any of our pre-war visits to the capital had been riotous successes. The people of Washington didn't strike me as being particularly theatre-minded.

Either that, or the pressure of State and international business was too much. Franklin D. Roosevelt paid a visit or two while we were there in 1937, and my wife and I received an invitation to visit the President and his wife at the White House. Unfortunately the letter with the invitation was handed in to the box office and did not get round to me until two days later—*exactly four hours after we were due.* I was later introduced to Eleanor Roosevelt by my good friend John Golden, but this was, once again, in Sardi's, not at the White House. The war was over—and Roosevelt was dead.

Just before sailing Isidore Godfrey and I were invited as principal guests of the Drama Desk of New York. This is a form of luncheon club to which notable personalities are invited each week. There are no speeches. Instead, the members of the club, consisting of the drama critics, film critics, and theatrical columnists from the New York papers, fire questions at the guests. I arrived a few minutes early at the restaurant where the luncheon was being held and sat chatting with Godfrey. Another gentleman came in and passed a casual remark about being early, and so we got into conversation. Shortly afterwards the secretary came in, saw us, and greeted us with "Oh, I see you all know one another." We explained we did not and were promptly introduced. The stranger and I both discovered we were talking to the one person we had really come to meet—the stranger being Brooks Atkinson, one of New York's leading critics. During all the years I had been going to New York I had known his name, as he had known mine, yet we had never met. Perhaps that has been a good thing —for me; up to date he has always been extremely good in his criticisms of me. Of the others that I had met, most of them have at some time or other given me at least a moderate slating. But as I've said elsewhere, that also can be a good thing, at any rate good *for* one.

That New York season of 1951 came to an end all too soon. As usual our cabin was full of people to see us off, and in some cases tears were not very far from the surface. It is a grand thing to know that one has good friends; friends that are going to miss one. That is one of the curses of travelling year in year out, as I have done for the past thirty years or more. Friends are made, and then for the rest of your life it is one constant round of saying good-by—and never quite knowing if and when you are likely to see them again. We sailed on the *Queen Elizabeth* at 2 A.M., Saturday, 3rd March.

As usual the company was persuaded to give a concert. Two, in fact: one to the cabin passengers and one to the saloon. I was asked if I would act as master of ceremonies at the concert in both cases and of course agreed. The night of the cabin concert was one of the stickiest of nights—from a weather point of view—and the ship had developed a pretty acute roll combined with a moderate pitching. As a combination calculated to add to the comfort of the passengers and keep seasickness at bay, it was not a one hundred per cent success. Several of the company were not feeling too well, and to make it possible for them to appear at the concert had resorted to the ship's doctor. Furthermore, the rolling of the ship was not conducive to the maintaining of a firm and erect stance. At any moment one was liable to make an involuntary journey to the ship's sides. This could, to a certain extent, be avoided by clinging firmly to the piano. If one did this, it was essential that one kept one's eyes glued to one of the more solid portions of the ship's structure, such as one of the pillars, otherwise the swaying and swinging of the looser portions, curtains, hanging lamps—the passenger audience themselves—had a peculiar effect on the eyes; that in turn could have a very disturbing effect on the stomach. But in spite of varying shades of green, rapidly growing more evident to the eye, the sufferers among the company, particularly those who had taken advantage of the doctor's potions, bore up bravely. After the ship had taken one terrific roll—just as I was about to announce an item, and during which I slid right to the ship's walls—our assistant musical director, one of the accompanists, leaned over and whispered in my ear a suggestion regarding my announcement of the next item. The moment came and I rose to my feet. Then, in the American style of commercial broadcasting (I was using a microphone for all announcements), I said:

"Ladies and gentlemen—this programme is coming to you by courtesy of Dramamine."

From the roar that went up I am convinced it is one of the funniest lines I have ever spoken. To William Cox-Ife, Assistant Musical Director—my grateful thanks. And, whether it was the sound of the word, the thoughts it conjured up in the minds of the suffering, or just the fact that the heartiness of their laughter had so suffused their checks, the fact remains that for the rest of the evening the varying shades of green gave way to rosy cheeks and healthy tan.

The night of the saloon concert the weather was far, far kinder. Sir Oliver Franks made the appeal for the Seamen's Charities—and I am pleased to say that the collection for those two concerts realized something approaching £200. The concert over, all repaired to the Verandah Cafe for food and drinks. One or two had asked me if it might be possible to meet Sir Oliver. I felt sure it would, told him, and asked him if he minded. His reply was—"But why only one or two? Can't I meet them all?"

The following day saw us in Southampton. Two weeks later we opened at Bournemouth for a two-week visit, followed by Oxford and Nottingham, each for two weeks. Then, after a further two weeks' rest—much-needed rest—we opened at the Savoy Theatre on Monday, 7th May, 1951, for the Festival of Britain season.

NINETEEN

Mix-ups

"*Don't you ever get the operas mixed up? I mean, do you ever* find yourself saying the words from another opera?" How often I have been asked that question! The answer is yes. I did once call another character by the name of a part she played in another opera. That is the only time, and it wasn't serious.

It was during the first act of *Patience*. Muriel Dickson was, I believe, playing the name part. At one point she trips onto the stage, humming lightly, sees Bunthorne (myself), turns, and begins to tiptoe off the stage. Bunthorne turns, sees and runs after her, takes her hand, and says, "Come hither, Patience." Unfortunately I said, "Come hither, Phyllis!" (Phyllis was Muriel's part in *Iolanthe*.) She stopped dead, turned with a look of amazement on her face, and cut into my line with a startled "It's Patience!" A very silly mistake on my part, and it could easily have ruined the opera. However, I recovered myself, the scene proceeded as per script, and no great harm was done.

It was otherwise with a principal tenor way back in the late teens and early twenties. I won't vouch for the truth of the story, although I knew James Hay, the tenor in question. I do not remember the name of the other character, nor do I recall ever having heard what opera was being performed at the time. The story, for what it is worth, is this: In several places in the operas lines similar to those in another opera occur, and in some places there is an exact repetition of words. Jimmy had reached one of these points and, his mind wandering slightly, slipped from the one opera into the other without realizing. The other character picked up the right cue for the wrong opera. Jimmy had a hazy idea that something was wrong but couldn't quite make out what, so he carried on. They had practically finished the scene when Jimmy realized what was wrong, stopped in the middle of a sentence, and said, "Dear, dear! I believe we're in the wrong opera!" and promptly started the whole scene again.

It is a good thing that audiences are, on the whole, a very tolerant race of people.

Things sometimes occur on the stage that may seem funny to the audience—but far from funny to the performer on the stage. I well remember one of those occasions that was a near tragedy to the performer in question, our principal tenor, Leo Darnton. We were in New York and the performance for the evening was *The Yeomen of the Guard*. Leo arrived in the theatre quite happily and cheerily informed us that he had had a nasty attack of hiccoughs—in fact he had only just got over them a few minutes before he entered the theatre. He completed his make-up, dressed, and went down to the stage for his first entrance—he was playing Fairfax. The moment came, and he walked onto the stage escorted by the four Tower Warders. The Lieutenant of the Tower, entering from the other side, spoke his first line:

"Halt! Colonel Fairfax, my old friend, we meet but sadly."

Leo, as Colonel Fairfax, stepped out from between the Warders, grasped the Lieutenant's hand, and in preparation for his first words, took in a breath that ended in a most explosive hiccough. A ripple of laughter went round the audience. Leo began to speak:

"Sir, I greet you with all good will (breath—hic); and I thank you for the zealous ca—(hic)—care with which you have guarded me from the pestilen—hic—tial dangers which threaten hic-man life outside."

By this time Leo was in such a state of nerves that the attack became so acute he was hiccoughing at every other word. The audience were almost in hysterics. Funny? Undoubtedly— from their point of view. From Leo's—no. Somehow or other he struggled through the scene; and somehow or other he managed to hiccough his way through his song and eventually make his way off the stage. By then he too had reached a state of hysteria—laughing, hiccoughing, crying, and swearing. He did not finish the show, his understudy being hurriedly prepared and dressed; nor did he appear the following evening—nor even the next. He still had hiccoughs.

When he did eventually reappear he was still nervous, and for a few moments after he made his first entrance—in this case as Nanki-Poo—we were all a little worried as to whether he would get through without a recurrence of the complaint. He did, of course, but I have been told that it was not outside the bounds of possibility for the memory of the hiccoughing occasion coupled with similar surroundings to have brought the complaint on again. Had that occurred it might have written a very definite finale to his career. However, it did not, and Leo eventually went to Australia, where he carried on singing Gilbert and Sullivan for many years. He is dead now. Were he not I probably would not tell the story for fear that the mere reminder of it might even now bring on an attack. Yes—it was very funny to the audience; it might have been a tragedy to the performer.

Another principal tenor we had with us in the days of the Small Company was Hughie Friel—a one hundred per cent Scotsman from Kilmarnock. His voice was pure gold; his accent pure Kilmarnock. Poor Hughie! Try as he would, he could never eliminate that accent.

Nevertheless, it was always a great joy for me to listen to him sing—for sing he could. And his sense of humour was never-failing. He knew he gave us a laugh, and knowing, laughed with us. And never will I forget his going to our stage manager and, with a dead serious face, asking him if, as he had some friends in front (we were in his home town of Kilmarnock), and they had specially requested it, he might sing "Afton Water" as an encore to "Sparkling Eyes." I shall always regret not having had a camera with me so that I could have recorded the look on the S. M.'s face for posterity.

Richard Walker was once the victim of one of the most embarrassing situations that can possibly happen on the stage. Walker had already given up the Poo-Bah roles that he had been playing for some years and had left the company when Charles Dorning was taken ill with appendicitis. The Sadler's Wells season was approaching and there was no one capable of carrying on with his roles, so Walker was approached and asked to return to the company for a special season and take over some of Dorning's parts. One of the parts was Archibald Grosvenor in *Patience*. Now, whereas Dorning was on the slim side, Walker was not, and the velvet costume of Grosvenor did not fit him as easily as it might—it was in fact skin tight, the breeches showing obvious strain. Everything went well up to the end of the first act, and even as far as the point where

Walker as Grosvenor sits on a stump in the second act for his song "The Magnet and the Churn." At the precise moment when he sat down the breeches gave up the unequal struggle and the back seam parted company.

Walker realized that something had happened, but was unable to determine what it was—and anyway, the show must go on. As the chorus ladies make their final exit the business calls for Grosvenor to follow them upstage and watch them off. As Walker did this, he necessarily turned his back on the audience, revealing to their startled gaze a vast expanse of white underwear. Naturally they laughed. The ladies having at last made their exit, Walker turned downstage again, and began to speak his own lines:

"At last they are gone! [Laughter] What is this mysterious fascination that I seem to exercise over all I come across? [Hearty laughter] A curse on my fatal beauty [hysterical laughter], for I am sick of conquests! [General collapse of the audience]"

Towards the end of the second act there is a scene between Grosvenor and Bunthorne (myself) wherein Grosvenor is told how he may escape the inconvenience of being madly loved at first sight by everyone he comes across. "Your personal appearance," says Bunthorne, "is highly objectionable to me."

"It is?" cries Grosvenor. "Oh, thank you, thank you! How can I express my gratitude?"

"By making a complete change at once," replies Bunthorne. "You must cut your hair, and *have a back parting.*"

I very much doubt if the audience heard another syllable of the remainder of the show.

To be "off"—that is to say, to fail to make an entrance onto the stage at the appropriate moment—is a professional crime of the first magnitude. I regret to say that I am not entirely innocent of that crime. There have been occasions when I have been well and truly "off," holding up the action and causing a hiatus or stage wait of as much as sixty seconds. Five seconds on the stage is a long time, so one can easily imagine what sixty must feel like. Generally speaking, those occasions are few. When they do occur, though, there is only one person responsible, and that is the culprit himself. It's no use making the excuse that the call-boy failed to call you, or that the loudspeaker system was out of order. It is up to you to anticipate any entrance, and to be on the side of the stage at least two minutes before you are due on.

I vividly recall three occasions on which a principal or principals were "off." In the first it was myself. One matinee at the Martin Beck Theatre during a performance of *The Mikado*, I had made my final exit in the first act, gone off to my dressing room, removed my black tunic, and donned my dressing gown. That done, I stretched out on my settee with the intention of taking a short nap—I had something like thirty minutes before I needed to re-dress for the second act—and gave strict instructions to my dresser to rouse me, should I have fallen into anything like a deep sleep, in plenty of time to dress and get onto the stage. The next thing I knew was Radley Flynn—the "Go-To," a part specially created for the bass singer in the Quartette (Madrigal), "Brightly dawns our wedding day"—shaking me by the shoulder and telling me I was "off." The fact that he had had time to get from the stage to my room—I should have made my entrance as he came off—waken me, help me into my costume and get me from my room to the stage will give you some idea of the length of the stage wait. Derek Oldham and Sylvia Cecil were the Nanki-Poo and Yum-Yum respectively, and by the time I reached the stage they were near hysterical panic. The audience were getting restless and were on the point of beginning that exasperating form of expressing their dissatisfaction—organized rhythmical hand-clapping—when I eventually appeared. An ironical cheer arose. As it happened, my very first line—a line I have found useful on several occasions—saved the day. I waited until they had finished cheering and there was a dead silence. Then I spoke:

"Oh, go on! Don't mind me!"

The whole atmosphere changed; the audience collapsed with laughter, and another thirty seconds was lost waiting for silence again. That obtained, I was only to discover that neither Derek nor Sylvia could speak a word, they being in an even worse condition than the audience. Tears were streaming down Derek's face as he openly and very audibly laughed; while Sylvia had rendered speech impossible by trying to swallow her laugh and only getting it halfway down.

But there was no excuse for me. I should not have run the risk of my dresser's forgetting to waken me.

The second occasion I recall concerned Sydney Granville—usually a most conscientious person, never allowing himself less than a full five minutes before an entrance was due. And the occasion of which I speak was no exception. The trio "Here's a how-de-do" (again the show was *The Mikado*) was over and Derek Oldham and I continued with the dialogue. I knew that Granny was on the side in plenty of time for his approaching entrance, as I had seen him there when I had made my various dashes around the backcloth during the encores to the trio, but when the moment came and I turned upstage with the remark "Now then, Lord Mayor, what is it?" on the tip of my tongue, he was not there. I turned and looked at Derek, but seeing the inevitable giggle coming over his face (Derek was the easiest man in the world to "dry up") I turned my back again, went further upstage, and looked off into the wings to see if I could see Pooh-Bah. There was no sign of him. It at once flashed through my mind that he had been taken sick—but the show must go on. Turning once again to Derek I spoke Poo-Bah's line, adapting it slightly to myself. Derek, miraculously, did not dry up. Instead, he spoke *my* next line. We went on in this way, adapting the lines as necessary, and I was just beginning to think that we had bridged the "wait" nicely when—Granville came on and began to speak his lines *from the beginning*. It was then I made the mistake. Quite audibly I said, "We've said all that!" So far as Derek was concerned, that was the last straw. He practically rolled on the stage in convulsions of laughter. Something clicked in Granny's mind—in a way, a kind of miracle, for Granny, as he would be the first to admit, had a one-track mind —and he cut the rest of the scene and went straight to the exit where he bumps Nanki-Poo off. For the sake of my American readers I do not mean that he "took him for a ride"—I mean that by a series of bumps with his padding-emphasized tummy, he more or less forcibly persuaded Derek to go "off" the stage. I learned later that Granny had been in the "wings" all the time engaged in conversation with the stage manager. They should both have known better.

The third occasion I recall was perhaps the worst of all. It was during the second act of *The Gondoliers*. Ella Halman as the Duchess of Plaza-Toro and I as the Duke had just finished the duet "Small titles and orders." Margaret Mitchell as Casilda was on the stage with us. As the duet comes to a close Marco and Giuseppe, the two apparent Kings of Barataria, played by

Leonard Osborne and Alan Styler, should make their entrance.

"Should" is the operative word, for there was neither sight nor sound of them. I began to "gag"—I went on "gagging," and still no sight of them. I moved across to the entrance from which they should appear. The side of the stage was utterly deserted. I crossed as rapidly as possible—still gagging—to the prompt corner intending to warn the call-boy. He was conspicuous by his absence; so, too, were the stage manager and the assistant stage manager. I recrossed the stage. One solitary stage hand had appeared there. I called out in a loud voice, as if it were all part of the script—"Boy! My compliments to Their Majesties and tell them we have arrived!" At that moment the stage manager arrived on the side, realized the situation, gasped, turned, and fled through the door off the stage and up the stairs to the dressing rooms, shouting as he went: "Kings! —you're OFF!" They were still in their dressing room—the call-boy having failed to call them—and their dressing room was three floors up.

In the meantime I tried to get Godfrey to take up the previous number again, but all I got was raised eyebrows and a shrug of the shoulders. I was just about to start telling a funny story when—clatter, clatter, clatter, crash (as the door to the stage burst open)—slam! (as it closed)—and two breathless Kings made their entrance.

Once more Gilbert had given me the right line:

"Ah! Their Majesties!"

The next few lines were never intended to sound as funny as they did, I'm sure.

Marco (Leonard Osborne): The (gasp, swallow) Duke of (gasp) Pla(swallow)za-Toro, I (gasp) believe.

Duke (myself): The same. Allow me to present—
Giuseppe (Alan Styler): The young (gasp, swallow, gasp) lady one of us (swallow, gasp) married! (gasp, swallow, phew!)
Casilda (Margaret Mitchell): Gentlemen, I am the (giggle) obedient servant of (smothered guffaw) one of you! (choke)

Gilbert must have writhed in his grave. Had such a thing happened while he was alive—well, I tremble to think of the upheaval that would have followed.

The call-boy's fault? Yes—up to a point. A moral? Yes. Never rely on the call-boy. In fact, never rely on anyone or anything. The final responsibility is the actor's own. If there is a lift or elevator to and from the dressing rooms, never use it, especially on the way down to the stage. It might get stuck. It once did, in Blackpool—and half of the chorus were off.

I have remarked a couple of times in a previous chapter how appropriate Gilbert can be, and has been, when at odd moments some unrehearsed incident has been followed by a line fitting whatever situation may have arisen. *Ruddigore* produced one such occasion. I had just made the entrance following on the duet between Despard and Mad Margaret and delivered my first line when the theatre cat, an extremely friendly beast, bounded onto the stage and proceeded to rub against my gaitered legs. I was unable to carry on with my lines for two reasons: one, I was utterly fascinated by the cat; and two, the feline addition to the cast struck the audience as amusing, which no doubt it was, even if only for being unexpected, and I had to wait for the laugh to subside. In the meantime I tried to encourage it to continue its journey across the stage and through the wings by administering a gentle pat on the rear end. But pussy thought the whole thing a marvellous joke and proceeded to claw, in a playful way, at my hand. I made a move to pick it up, but pussy was not having any. She scampered away, keeping just out of my reach. There was nothing to do but to assume as dignified an attitude as possible, wait for silence, and carry on as if nothing had happened. Silence at last descended and I spoke my next line:

"This visit is unexpected!"

The resultant roar of laughter achieved what I with all my persuasion had been unable to. Pussy reached the wings in one wild leap.

Another instance in New York came after the encore to the Madrigal quartette in *The Mikado*. Derek Oldham, Sylvia Cecil, Marjorie Eyre, and, I believe, Leslie Rands were the singers, and so well had they sung it that although I, as Ko-Ko, made my usual entrance following the encore, the audience would have none of me and demanded a second encore. That over, I again entered, and again it looked as if they were going to demand a further encore. However, I stood my ground and waited for silence. Then I spoke my first line:

"Oh, go on—don't mind me!"

Items of news do not escape. Back in the 1930's, it may be remembered, "incidents" were taking place with monotonous regularity in Hong Kong, each incident being followed by an apology from Japan. One day practically every paper in the Kingdom came out with a big headline on the front page— one of *Pictorial Daily's* going so far as to cut its pictures in half, devoting the top of the page to the words *JAPAN APOLO-GISES AGAIN*. That night Darrell Fancourt, as the Mikado, said to Ko-Ko, "My poor fellow, . . . you've beheaded the heir to the throne of Japan." Ko-Ko replied: "I beg to offer an unqualified apology."

Bertha Lewis once found herself the centre of an embar-

rassing situation on the stage. The show was *Patience*, and
Bertha made her entrance for the first act finale. As she moved
downstage several of the chorus behind her began to titter.
Some of the girls made a move towards her, and one actually
began to fumble at the back of her frock. Bertha heard all this,
felt the fumbling, and was furious. Making a majestic turn upstage with the object of quieting the titterers, she gave her back
to the audience, and a mighty roar went up. She swept round
again, realizing that something was wrong in the rear. Her
hand went behind her back to discover that on rising from her
chair in her dressing room she had inadvertently got her corsets
hooked onto the back of her frock. One line was introduced
into the part of Lady Jane that Gilbert never wrote—"My
God!"

Patience was also the scene of an incident that raised my
opinion of a woman's courage to one of complete and sincere
admiration. Alan Styler, the Grosvenor, was seated on his
stump singing "The Magnet and the Churn"; the girls—the
rapturous maidens—were lying on the floor, chins cupped in
their hands, listening intently. An outsize in rats appeared at
one side of the stage. Several, and eventually all, saw it, and
their eyes opened wide—but the rapturous expression did not
leave their faces—not even when that rat actually ran over the
legs of one and the back of another girl, from whence it made
its way into the flats and finally disappeared down a hole. I
loathe rats, and I am sure that if I had been on the stage myself
I would have been so petrified with fright that I would have
been unable to speak. Not so the girls—not one of them faltered
in word, note, or gesture. A medal should be struck for courage
like that.

I would not, of course, under any circumstances, refer to

the time when one small baby mouse cleared a whole dressing room. How he got into the ladies' room I know not, because originally he was mine. I think he lived somewhere just behind the point where my make-up basket stood on the floor, for at odd moments, when I was seated quietly in my chair, resting between scenes or acts, he would pop up onto the top of the basket, eye me quizzically for a moment, and then sit up on his hind legs and proceed to curl his whiskers. I am not fond of mice, either, but I got quite fond of that little fellow. I think it was his cheek I admired. He reminded me of India—not that I liked him for that, unless it was that in reminding me of the place he was also reminding me that it was several thousand miles away. But he did bring to mind my five likable companions that shared my quarters with me: one mouse, one small ant-eater, and three lizards—Momma, Poppa, and the "chotta chappie"—a very baby lizard who lived in my desk drawer. The mouse was the only useless one of the quintette, but, like my friend of the dressing room, I admired his cheek.

I am frequently asked—"How do you learn those terrible tongue-twisting songs—the Major General's and the Nightmare Song?" and "Which is your favourite part?" To the first the answer is "I don't know." And that is absolutely true. I have no set plan for learning a song or a part—they sort of grow on me. This much I do know, that once I become conscious of the fact that I am singing them, consciously conscious, I mean, then I can say good-by to reaching a successful conclusion— for I am bound to fluff. No, it is not that I become automatic in my singing. I must know what I am singing, or saying, otherwise it would become meaningless—it is just that I must not be conscious of knowing. "I hope," as Ralph Rackstraw says to Josephine, "I make myself clear, lady!"

264 · *Here's a How-de-do*

As to the second question, it is a very difficult one to answer, and I have invariably given the answer "I haven't got one." That is not quite true, but the difficulty is to discover which it is. As soon as I settle on one I find that there is something in another that makes me feel that after all that is my favourite. And so it goes on. Naturally Jack Point comes very near the top—it must be by virtue of the part itself and the tremendous acting possibilities it holds. He is such a very human person. But so is Ko-Ko. And the Lord Chancellor is one of the most likable people. King Gama again, though a short part as parts go, is chockablock with possibilities, whereas Bunthorne gives the opportunity of giving one's satirical senses full play—and so on, and so on. I think my first answer was the correct one, with perhaps the qualification of admitting a sneaking regard for King Gama, Jack Point, and the Lord Chancellor. Sir Joseph Porter, mind you, has much to commend him, and the Duke of Plaza-Toro—but there, I'm off again. My favourite part? The one I am about to play next—unless I'm playing it at the moment.

I may have an opportunity to supply some proof myself, for since my resignation from the D'Oyly Carte organization I have been approached many times by S. M. Chartock to join his Gilbert and Sullivan company.

Mr. Chartock has been associated with the professional presentation of Gilbert and Sullivan for some years now, and he is, I have every reason to believe, most sincere in his efforts to present them in as pure a form as possible. Incidentally, he put on a short season in New York in 1949–50 out of which I received some of the best notices I have ever had—in spite of the fact that I was in England at the time!

That was not his first venture into New York with Gilbert and Sullivan. I possess programmes, sent to me by friends, of his production of *The Mikado* in 1936 with such veterans of the American Gilbert and Sullivan stage as William Danforth, Frank Moulan, Herbert Watrous, Vivian Hart, and Vera Ross. It is also interesting to note that among the "Ladies of the Mikado's Suite" was Marion Ross, of whom I have spoken elsewhere.

As to Mr. Chartock's offer, I can only quote Captain Corcoran: "Time alone can tell."

English friends often ask whether Americans really like Gilbert and Sullivan. There is but one answer to that—Yes. If proof were needed, the success and popularity of the Blue Hill Troupe, the Ridgewood (N.J.) Gilbert and Sullivan Opera Company, and all the other amateur operatic societies that produce one or another of the operas with clocklike regularity every year could supply it.

TWENTY

First Act Curtain

I don't think I have ever felt so nervous before a show as I was that opening night of the Festival season, not even on that opening night of the 1932–33 Savoy season when Rupert D'Oyly Carte had announced me as the chosen successor to Harry Lytton.

In this 1951 season we opened with *The Mikado*. My—Ko-Ko's—opening song is not so terrifying in itself as Major-General Stanley's, but on this occasion we were broadcasting the first act. On the stage a fluff is bad enough; a forgotten word is frightening, but it can be covered by some piece of visual business; a stage wait of the shortest possible seems like minutes. But on the air, no visual business can be seen, and that shortest possible stage wait becomes an eternity, all of which promptly creates a panic in the mind. Can you remember your lines? You begin to shake, you begin to dither, you are a jelly. Added to that you know that all the past members of the D'Oyly Carte Opera Company who are able will be in front.

On top of which Winston Churchill was in the box occupied on that previous occasion by Harry Lytton. I don't think Winston Churchill's presence would have worried me quite so much had it not been for the third verse of my first song—"A little list . . . of society offenders . . . who never would be missed"—which alludes to those ". . . apologetic statesmen, of a compromising kind,"

> Such as—What d'ye call him—Thing'em-bob, and likewise—well—never mind,
> And 'St-'st-'st and What's-his-name, and also—well, You-know-who—.

I knew very well that the point would not be missed by the audience—but—I naturally did not want to make any gesture, give any inflection to word or line, or suggest by a look that he—Churchill—would be among those who "never would be missed." As I suspected, the first of those lines brought a roar; when I reached the words "never mind" there was a further and bigger roar, and so far I had managed to achieve my object. Then it came to me. Why I hadn't realized before, as I should have done, that Gilbert never lets one down, I don't know. "And 'St-'st-'st, and What's-his-name," I sang, then—one quick look at "Winnie" as I continued—"and also—well—You-know-who!" Never have I heard such an explosion of laughter. The expression goes "the house fell in," and for a moment I was almost afraid that it would. Malcolm, in the pit, doubled up and very nearly forgot to carry on conducting, while I am told that "Winnie" himself very nearly fell out of the box.

No—Gilbert never lets one down. Did I hear a wee small echo saying "What, never?" I refuse to quote Gilbert any further, and repeat "Never."

All my nervousness disappeared—the butterflies in my stomach ceased to flutter round. How could one feel nervous in the face of such enthusiasm?

Some weeks later, though, during another performance of *The Mikado*, I suffered a slight mental aberration during the singing of "Titwillow." I had reached the final verse (it was at a Saturday matinee) and sang the first line quite correctly. For some unknown reason I continued with the second line of the second verse; I realized what I had done, but the difficulty was to get back to the third-verse words again. I had to do a bit of blah-blahing before I could, then, having managed it, completed it correctly. At a matinee every endeavour is made to cut encores wherever possible, and it was usually possible to cut any encore to "Titwillow." Ella Halman, as Katisha, crossed over to me and was about to carry on with the dialogue, but, before she could speak, a voice from the gallery called out:

"Sing it again—and let's hear the right words this time!"

It is sometimes unfortunate for a performer to achieve a reputation, as I have done, for clarity of diction—especially when the audience in front know every word of what you are supposed to be singing. That cry from the gallery immediately set the remainder of the house clapping again; Ella's words could not be heard—and I had to do it.

But I do not think I shall permit my clarity of diction to suffer just on account of that. Speaking of diction reminds me of an occasion when I was having lunch in the Lambs Club in New York. One of the members came and sat down at the table around which several of us were already seated. He was looking rather grim and was asked: "What's the trouble?"

"It's this new show I'm rehearsing," he told us. "I'm turning the part in."

"What!" exclaimed another. "But I thought you told me it was one of the best parts you'd ever had."

"Maybe," he replied, "but some of the lines are too blue. I've asked to have them cut out, or altered, or something—but nothing doing. 'No' says they, 'those lines stay right in the script.'"

An old actor, who up to this moment had not apparently been taking much notice of the conversation, looked up and said:

"But you don't want to turn in a good part just because some of the lines are a bit blue. When you reach the bad ones, don't speak 'em properly—just mumble 'em, laddie—just mumble 'em."

"Ah!" exclaimed a young fellow at the end of the table who had not spoken a word till then, "Now I understand: actors should be obscene, and not heard!"

But to return to the Festival season. From my point of view it was a season of hard work. Not just the hard work of performing my roles in the theatre. Richard Watson had announced his intention of retiring from the company as far back as January or February when we were in the United States. Someone had to be found to replace him, the choice eventually falling upon Fisher Morgan. He had to be rehearsed and finally given some performances. On several occasions Ella Halman stepped down in favour of a new Katisha, or a Duchess or a Lady Jane, etc., and so—more rehearsals. There was also some degree of sickness. Darrell Fancourt did not open the season, as he should have done, in the role of the Mikado. It was some three weeks before he rejoined the cast, having had to have a very serious operation on one eye, an operation that necessitated its removal.

All this meant not only a deal of extra work, but an added nervous strain, especially in respect of the newcomers going on for parts for the first time. If they had been properly rehearsed, it would perhaps not have been too bad. For their being under-rehearsed there is, I suppose, some excuse. So much had to be done that there was insufficient time. But for their being badly rehearsed there is no excuse. It is to their own personal credit that they managed to get through the shows without upsetting the general balance too much. But it is nerve-racking to others on the stage with them. It's rather like playing two parts simultaneously.

On the whole, though, I feel it must be reckoned a successful season. With the exception of the mid-week matinee the theatre was booked solid for the whole of the season, and as usual queues were forming on the Friday night for the last performance on Saturday, 4th August.

Following the general practice, the show to be performed was kept a secret even from the cast until a very short while before the curtain rose, and again as usual, it was not one complete show, but one act of one opera, one of another—in this case the first act of *The Gondoliers* and the second act of *The Mikado*. This gives every member of the cast the opportunity of appearing. It was known to the public generally by this time that Ella Halman, Richard Watson, Margaret Mitchell, and I would not be returning to the company when it reassembled for its next tour six weeks later, and the respective successors to Richard Watson and myself were given the parts in *The Gondoliers*. The successors to Ella and Margaret, apparently, were not ready to go on.

It was a sad occasion in many respects, but I confess I managed to get a couple of laughs out of it. The first was on my initial entrance. In the second act I more or less slide onto the

stage with no build-up; but as I went on I was greeted with a terrific reception. It was flattering, it was touching, and for a moment I was overcome to the extent of having to swallow very hard—I would have blinked the tear out of my eye had I not remembered the mascara round my eyes in time. I waited until the applause subsided and spoke my first line—my first line of the evening: "Oh, go on—don't mind me!" Yum-Yum gave me her reply:

"I'm afraid we're distressing you."

"Never mind," speaking my next line, "I must get used to it."

I was struck by the appropriateness of the lines and the touch of irony that went with them. How they struck the audience I do not know except that roars of laughter greeted both. I had to laugh myself.

In the days of Henry Lytton it had been the custom for him to step forward at the end of the last performance in any town or city and make a short speech of thanks, acknowledging our reception and, towards the end of his career with the company, saying a few words about himself. When he retired this custom was at once stopped. During the course of the evening the General Manager, Alfred Nightingale, came to my room to tell me that it had been decided to break with the new "tradition" and I was to make a short speech.

The curtain at length came down for the last time. The show was over, the season at an end, and more than one member of the company had reached the parting of the ways.

I had expected to see something of Miss Bridget D'Oyly Carte during that last performance, even if only in passing. I was informed later that she was not in the theatre, in fact was not in town—she had gone away to the country for the week-end. I confess to some feeling of surprise. I must also confess to finding her, in all my contacts with her, a very charming person. A little vague at times, perhaps, and somewhat shy of talking business—certainly of talking money.

I joined the D'Oyly Carte Opera Company in 1922, remaining with them until 1939, when my connection with them was brought to an abrupt end by the war. I rejoined them in 1946 after my return from the Royal Air Force and remained with them until 1951. On the whole my years with them have been happy enough, and I owe them a debt of gratitude for having given me the opportunities they have. Those few facts, coupled with the circumstances related earlier, make Miss Bridget D'Oyly Carte's last letter to me all the more surprising. I quote from it:

Dear Mr. Green,
    Thank you for the work you have done. . . .
    I am indeed sorry that you have *never apparently been able to settle down really happily with us for long* for I feel that you could have so well have done had you wished.

                                        Yours very sincerely,
                                        Bridget D'Oyly Carte.

The italics are mine.

My twenty-two years of active connection with the D'Oyly Carte Opera Company were, on the whole, very happy years —in spite of anything that may be suggested to the contrary. During those years I have made many friends, the vast majority of whom I have never met, nor can ever hope to meet, both in England and in the United States. I am grateful to them, for without them I could never have achieved a tenth part of any success I may have had. A few of those friends have known me off the stage as well as on; a few more of them have been able to penetrate my disguise as I left the theatre—the disguise of being without make-up; but the majority have known me only as Sir Joseph or Ko-Ko, Bunthorne or the Lord Chancellor, Jack Point or King Gama, Robin Oakapple or Major-General Stanley, the Duke of Plaza-Toro, or John Wellington Wells.

Many is the time I have walked out from the stage door right through a crowd of people waiting for autographs without being recognized—and have sometimes been asked if Mr. Green has left the theatre. I was always grateful for this for three reasons: one, I was always very hot when leaving the theatre and liked to avoid standing about in the chill of the night air—I once contracted a very bad attack of laryngitis and was off for a week through it, one of the few times I have been off through sickness; two, it always embarrassed me, strange as it may seem; and three, I am a great believer in preserving, as far as is possible, the mystery of the theatre.

When I was touring in the George Edwardes Company of *Sybil* an aunt of mine expressed the desire to come backstage after a performance she was to see. I agreed, and told her to ask for me at the stage door. I had not had time to remove my make-up before she arrived. That was the first of the shocks she had (she had never been backstage before in her life, though quite a theatregoer). Then I took her onto the stage, in accordance with her wishes. Her disappointment was intense.

"Oh," she exclaimed, "I don't think I want to come to a theatre again. When you came on first I could see the sledge you had just got out of. Now I know you just walked down that passage. All the mystery has gone. And—that horrible stuff you have on your face!"

It is impossible for actors today to maintain the complete mystery, I know, but I still think it is a pity.

Most theatregoers are content to leave the theatre at the end of a performance and retain the illusion of the play they have just seen, and the characters in it. It is the fans and the bobbysoxers only who clamour round the stage doors and help to make life more difficult for the actor, especially those who acquire terrific "crushes" on the poor creature. They can, and do, make life miserable. They are few in comparison— but however few they are, they are too many.

Over a period of years it is inevitable that some differences of opinion, quarrels, etc., should arise. The very nature of the work, throwing actors and producers into constant and close contact with each other for long periods at a time, makes it so. Nevertheless, I have enjoyed my work, have never quarrelled with it, and, to the best of my belief, have never taken a personal difference onto the stage.

In the years since I first performed Gilbert and Sullivan I have experienced most of the emotions that man is prone to: great happiness; great sorrow; tremendous elation and intense depression; hope and despair; pleasure, regret. Of the last I have but few. If I had my life to live over again I think I would spend it, with but few exceptions, as I have—singing and performing Gilbert and Sullivan—unless it had been performing Shakespeare. I say I think, because, unless one is a seer and can look into the future, it is difficult to say what one would do, but of this I am pretty certain—I would have spent it on the stage.

Yes, in spite of what anyone may say to the contrary, I have been very happy. Then why did I leave? That, I am afraid,

is a long story. My leaving was inevitable—if not now, then at some not too distant date. Some day perhaps, when conditions change, I may once again perform some of those wonderful roles in England. It remains but for me to say two things, and to say them I would like to quote first from the second show in which I set foot on the professional stage—*The Maid of the Mountains:*

> "Farewell, the old familiar ties are broken—
>
> . . . .
>
> My old friends—farewell!"

Second—I trust I do not find my way into Ko-Ko's little list!

Index